the voice of Matthew

Lauren F. Winner

A SCRIPTURE PROJECT TO REDISCOVER THE STORY OF THE BIBLE

THOMAS NELSON
Since 1798

NASHVILLE DALLAS MEXICO CITY RIO DE JANEIRO BEIJING

www.thomasnelson.com

The Voice of Matthew

Published in Nashville, TN, by Thomas Nelson. Thomas Nelson is a trademark of Thomas Nelson, Inc.

Published in association with Eames Literary Services, Nashville, Tennessee

Typesetting by Brecca Theele

Printed in the United States of America

2 3 4 5 6 7 8 9—15 14 13 12 11 10 09 08 07

Contributors

The Voice of Matthew

Scriptures retold by:
LAUREN WINNER

Scholarly review by:
DAVID CAPES
PETER DAVIDS

Editorial review by:
Maleah Bell
James F. Couch, Jr.
Marilyn Duncan
Amanda Haley
Kelly Hall
Merrie Noland
and Chris Seay

the voice.
A Scripture project to rediscover the story of the Bible

The Gospel According to Matthew

Appendices

the voice.

A Scripture project to rediscover the story of the Bible

Any literary project reflects the age in which it is written. ***The Voice*** is created for and by a church in great transition. Throughout the body of Christ, extensive discussions are ongoing about a variety of issues including style of worship, how we separate culture from our theology, and what is essential truth. In fact, we are struggling with what is truth. At the center of this discussion is the role of Scripture. This discussion is heating up with strong words being exchanged. Instead of furthering the division over culture and theology, it is time to bring the body of Christ together again around the Bible. Thomas Nelson, Inc., and Ecclesia Bible Society together are developing Scripture products that foster spiritual growth and theological exploration out of a heart for worship and mission. We have dedicated ourselves to hearing and proclaiming God's voice through this project.

Previously most Bibles and biblical reference works were produced by professional scholars writing in academic settings. ***The Voice*** uniquely represents collaboration among scholars, pastors, writers, musicians, poets, and other artists. The goal is to create the finest Bible products to help believers experience the joy and wonder of God's revelation. Four key words describe the vision of this project:

- holistic   considers heart, soul, and mind
- beautiful   achieves literary and artistic excellence
- sensitive   respects cultural shifts and the need for accuracy
- balanced   includes theologically diverse writers and scholars

Uniqueness of The Voice

About 40 different human authors are believed to have been inspired by God to write the Scriptures. ***The Voice*** retains the perspective of the human writers. Most English translations attempt to even out the styles of the different authors in sentence structure and vocabulary. Instead, ***The Voice*** distinguishes sentence structure and vocabulary of each author. The heart of the project is retelling the story of the Bible in a form that is as fluid as modern literary works yet that remains true to the original manuscripts. First, accomplished writers create an English rendering; then, respected Bible scholars adjust the rendering to align the manuscript with the original texts. Attention is paid to the use of idioms, artistic elements, confusion of pronouns, repetition of conjunctives, modern sentence structure, and the public reading of the passage. In the process, the writer or scholar may adjust the arrangement of words or expand the phrasing to create an English equivalent.

To help the reader understand how the new rendering of a passage compares to the original manuscripts, several indicators are imbedded within the text. Italic type indicates words not directly tied to a dynamic translation of the original language. Material delineated by a screened box or set apart in a box expands on the theme. This portion is not taken directly from the original language. To avoid the endless repetition of simple conjunctives, dialog is formatted as a screenplay. The speaker is indicated, the dialog is indented, and quotation marks are not used. This helps greatly in the public reading of Scripture. Sometimes the original text includes exposition that interrupts the dialog. This is shown either as a stage direction immediately following the speaker's name or as part of the narrative section that immediately precedes the speaker's name. The screenplay format clearly shows who is speaking.

Throughout ***The Voice,*** other language devices improve readability. We follow the standard conventions used in most translations regarding textual evidence. ***The Voice*** is based on the earliest and best manuscripts from the original languages (Greek, Hebrew, and Aramaic). When significant variations influence a reading, we follow the publishing standard by bracketing the passage and placing a note in the margin or at the bottom of the page while maintaining the traditional chapter and verse divisions. The footnotes reference quoted material and help the reader understand the translation for a particular word. Words that are borrowed from another language or words that are not common outside of the theological community (such as baptism, repentance, and salvation) are translated into more common terminology. For clarity, some pronouns are replaced with their antecedents. Word order and parts of speech are sometimes altered to help the reader understand the original passage.

— Ecclesia Bible Society

About *The Voice* Project

As retold, edited, and illustrated by a gifted team of writers, scholars, poets, and storytellers

A New Way to Process Ideas

Chris Seay's vision for ***The Voice*** goes back 15 years to his early attempts to teach the Bible in the narrative as the story of God. As western culture has moved into what is now referred to as postmodernism, Chris observed that the way a new generation processes ideas and information raises obstacles to traditional methods of teaching biblical content. His desire has grown to open the Bible in ways that overcome these obstacles to people coming to faith. Instead of propositional-based thought patterns, people today are more likely to interact with events and individuals through complex observations involving emotions, cognitive processes, tactile experiences, and spiritual awareness. Much as in the parables of Jesus and in the metaphors of the prophets, narrative communication touches the whole person.

Hence, out of that early vision comes the need in a postmodern culture to present Scripture in a narrative form. The result is a retelling of the Scriptures: ***The Voice***, not of words, but of meaning and experience.

The Timeless Narrative

The Voice is a fresh expression of the timeless narrative known as the Bible. Stories that were told to emerging generations of God's goodness by their grandparents and tribal leaders were recorded and assembled to form the Christian Scriptures. Too often, the passion, grit, humor, and beauty has been lost in the translation process. ***The Voice*** seeks to recapture what was lost.

From these early explorations by Chris and others has come ***The Voice***: a Scripture project to rediscover the story of the Bible. Thomas

Nelson, Inc., and Ecclesia Bible Society have joined together to stimulate unique creative experiences and to develop Scripture products and resources to foster spiritual growth and theological exploration out of a heart for the mission of the church and worship of God.

Traditional Translations

Putting the Bible into the language of modern readers has too often been a painstaking process of correlating the biblical languages to the English vernacular. The Bible is filled with passages intended to inspire, captivate, and depict beauty. The old school of translation most often fails at attempts to communicate beauty, poetry, and story. ***The Voice*** is a collage of compelling narratives, poetry, song, truth, and wisdom. ***The Voice*** will call you to enter into the whole story of God with your heart, soul, and mind.

A New Retelling

One way to describe this approach is to say that it is a "soul translation," not just a "mind translation." But "translation" is not the right word. It is really the retelling of the story. The "retelling" involves translation and paraphrase, but mostly entering into the story of the Scriptures and recreating the event for our culture and time. It doesn't ignore the role of scholars, but it also values the role of writers, poets, songwriters, and artists. Instead, teams of scholars partner with a writer to blend the mood and voice of the original author with an accurate rendering of words of the text in English.

The Voice is unique in that it represents collaboration among scholars, writers, musicians, and other artists. Its goal is to create the finest Bible products to help believers experience the joy and wonder of God's revelation. In this time of great transition within the church, we are seeking to give gifted individuals opportunities to craft a variety of products and experiences: a translation of the Scriptures, worship music, worship film festivals, biblical art, worship conferences, gatherings of creative thinkers, a Web site for individuals and churches to share biblical resources, and books derived from exploration during the Bible translation work.

The heart of each product within ***The Voice*** project is the retelling of the Bible story. To accomplish the objectives of the project and to facilitate the various products envisioned within the project, the Bible text is being translated. We trust that this retelling will be a helpful contribution to a fresh engagement with Scripture. The Bible is the greatest story ever told, but it often doesn't read like it. ***The Voice*** brings the biblical narratives to life and reads more like a great novel than the traditional versions of the Bible that are seldom opened in contemporary culture.

Readable and Enjoyable

A careful process is being followed to assure that the spiritual, emotional, and artistic goals of the project are met. First, the retelling of the Bible has been designed to be readable and enjoyable by emphasizing the narrative nature of Scripture. Beyond simply providing a set of accurately translated individual words, phrases, and sentences, our teams were charged to render the biblical texts with sensitivity to the flow of the unfolding story. We asked them to see themselves not only as guardians of the sacred text, but also as storytellers, because we believe that the Bible has always been intended to be heard as the sacred story of the people of God. We assigned each literary unit (for example, the writings of John or Paul) to a team that included a skilled writer and biblical and theological scholars, seeking to achieve a mixture of scholarly expertise and literary skill.

Personal and Diverse

Second, as a consequence of this team approach, ***The Voice*** is both personal and diverse. God used about 40 human instruments to communicate His message, and each one has a unique voice or literary style. Standard translations tend to flatten these individual styles so that each book reads more or less like the others—with a kind of impersonal textbook-style prose. Some translations and paraphrases have paid more attention to literary style—but again, the literary style of one writer, no matter how gifted, can unintentionally obscure the diversity of the original voices. To address these problems, we asked our teams to try to feel and convey the diverse literary styles of the original authors.

Faithful

Third, we have taken care that ***The Voice*** is faithful and that it avoids prejudice. Anyone who has worked with translation and paraphrase knows that there is no such thing as a completely unbiased or objective translation. So, while we do not pretend to be purely objective, we asked our teams to seek to be as faithful as possible to the biblical message as they understood it together. In addition, as we partnered biblical scholars and theologians with our writers, we intentionally built teams that did not share any single theological tradition. Their diversity has helped each of them not to be trapped within his or her own individual preconceptions, resulting in a faithful and fresh rendering of the Bible.

Stimulating and Creative

Fourth, we have worked hard to make ***The Voice*** both stimulating and creative. As we engaged the biblical text, we realized again and again that certain terms have conventional associations for modern readers that would not have been present for the original readers—and that the original readers would have been struck by certain things that remain invisible or opaque to modern readers. Even more, we realized that modern readers from different religious or cultural traditions would hear the same words differently. For example, when Roman Catholic or Eastern Orthodox readers encounter the word "baptism," a very different set of meanings and associations come to mind than those that would arise in the minds of Baptist or Pentecostal readers. And a secular person encountering the text would have still different associations. The situation is made even more complex when we realize that *none* of these associations may resemble the ones that would have come to mind when John invited Jewish peasants and Pharisees into the water of the Jordan River in the months before Jesus began His public ministry. It is far harder than most people realize to help today's readers recapture the original impact of a single word like "baptism." In light of this challenge, we decided, whenever possible, to select words that would stimulate fresh thinking rather than reinforce unexamined assumptions. We want the next generation of Bible readers—whatever their background—to have the best opportunity possible to hear God's message the way the first generation of Bible readers heard it.

Transformative

Finally, we desire that this translation will be useful and transformative. It is all too common in many of our Protestant churches to have only a few verses of biblical text read in a service, and then that selection too often becomes a jumping-off point for a sermon that is at best peripherally related to, much less rooted in, the Bible itself. The goal of ***The Voice*** is to promote the public reading of longer sections of Scripture—followed by thoughtful engagement with the biblical narrative in its richness and fullness and dramatic flow. We believe the Bible itself, in all its diversity and energy and dynamism, is the message; it is not merely the jumping-off point.

The various creations of the project bring creative application of commentary and interpretive tools. These are clearly indicated and separated from the Bible text that is drawn directly from traditional sources. Along with the creative resources and fresh expressions of God's Word, the reader has the benefit of centuries of biblical research applied dynamically to our rapidly changing culture.

The products underway in ***The Voice*** include dynamic and interactive presentations of the critical passages in the life of Jesus and the early church, recorded musical presentation of Scripture originally used in worship or uniquely structured for worship, artwork commissioned from young artists, dramatized audio presentations from the Gospels and the Old Testament historical books, film commentary on our society using the words of Scripture, and exploration of the voice of each human author of the Bible.

The first product for ***The Voice***, entitled ***The Last Eyewitness: The Final Week,*** released Spring 2006, follows Jesus through His final week of life on earth through the firsthand account of John the apostle. This book combines the drama of the text with the artwork of Rob Pepper into a captivating retelling of Jesus' final days. The second product, ***The Dust Off Their Feet: Lessons from the First Church,*** was released September 2006 and includes the entire Book of Acts retold by Brian McLaren with commentary and articles written by nine scholars and pastors.

Forthcoming projects include ***Eyewitness Live***, an audio dramatization of the Gospel of John; ***The Voice of Luke***, in which Luke sets the record straight with a doctor's analytical mind; and ***Song of Love*** by Donald Miller and Lauren Winner, a fresh retelling of Song of Solomon and Ecclesiastes.

The Team

The team writing ***The Voice*** brings unprecedented gifts to this unique project. An award-winning fiction writer, an acclaimed poet, a pastor renowned for using art and narrative in his preaching and teaching, Greek and Hebrew authorities, and biblical scholars are all coming together to capture the beauty and diversity of God's Word.

Writers

The writer for ***The Voice*** who has contributed to ***The Voice of Matthew*** is:

- **Lauren Winner**—This former book editor for *Beliefnet* is author of *Girl Meets God, Mudhouse Sabbath*, and *Real Sex: the Naked Truth about Chastity,* and she is a contributor to *5 Paths to the Love of Your*

Life. Lauren has degrees from Columbia and Cambridge universities and has her doctorate in the history of American religion.

The two critical reviewers of ***The Voice of Matthew*** are:

- **David Capes, PhD**—Chair of the Department of Christianity and Philosophy at Houston Baptist University. He has written several books, including *The Footsteps of Jesus in the Holy Land*.
- **Peter H. Davids, PhD**—Adjunct Professor at Tyndale Theological Amsterdam, International Teams Innsbrook, and resident scholar at Basileia Vineyard Bern. He is author of *James* and *1 & 2 Peter and Jude* in the *New International Commentary on the New Testament* and editor of the *Dictionary of Late New Testament and Its Development*.

Other writers for ***The Voice,*** who are working on forthcoming products, include:

Eric Bryant—pastor/author
David Capes—professor/author
Tara Leigh Cobble—singer/songwriter
Don Chaffer—singer/songwriter/poet
Lori Chaffer—singer/songwriter/poet
Robert Creech—pastor/author
Greg Garrett— professor/author
Christena Graves—singer
Sara Groves—singer/songwriter
Amanda Haley—biblical archaeologist/editor
Charlie Hall—singer/songwriter
Kelly Hall—editor/poet
Justin Hyde—pastor/author
Andrew Jones— pastor/consultant
E. Chad Karger—counselor/author/pastor

Tim Keel—pastor
Greg LaFollette—musician/songwriter
Evan Lauer—pastor/author
Phuc Luu—chaplain/adjunct instructor
Christian McCabe—pastor/artist
Brian McLaren—pastor/author
Donald Miller—author
Sean Palmer—pastor
Jonathan Hal Reynolds—poet
Robbie Seay, singer/songwriter
Kerry Shook—pastor
Chuck Smith, Jr.—pastor/author
Allison Smythe—poet
Leonard Sweet—author
Kristin Swenson—professor/author
Phyllis Tickle—author
Seth Woods—singer/songwriter
Dieter Zander—pastor/author

Scholars

Other biblical and theological scholars for ***The Voice*** include:

Darrell L. Bock, PhD—professor
Alan Culpepper, PhD—dean/professor
Creig Marlowe, PhD—dean/professor
Jack Wisdom, JD—lawyer
Nancy de Claissé Walford, PhD—professor
Dave Garber, PhD—professor
Joseph Blair, ThD—professor
Kenneth Waters, Sr., PhD—professor
Peter Rhea Jones, Sr., PhD—pastor/professor
Sheri Klouda, PhD—professor
Troy Miller, PhD—professor

Felisi Sorgwe, PhD—pastor/professor
Chuck Pitts, PhD—professor

Artists

Art and images will be incorporated into many of the products that will provide a visual reference, source of meditation, and convey the splendor of God's story that cannot be captured in words. The first book, *The Last Eyewitness: The Final Week* contains numerous illustrations by Rob Pepper, an accomplished British artist.

Musicians

The passages meant for use in worship are being set to music with a number of music albums planned. The recordings themselves are experiences of collaboration and worship. A large studio was selected to allow up to 20 musicians to perform live, creating a truly dynamic sound. Most of the featured artists participated in many of the songs, making a diverse and rich sound. The spirit of the retelling of the story found in ***The Voice*** comes through in this unique collection of songs in a variety of styles and moods. The first CD, *Songs from the Voice, Vol. 1, Please Don't Make Us Sing This Song*, contains 13 original songs inspired by selected psalms from ***The Voice.*** The second CD, *Songs from the Voice, Vol. 2,* features music drawn from the same Scripture selections as *Handel's Messiah* and the unique retelling about Messiah in ***The Voice***. The featured artists are:

Tyler Burkum
Tara Leigh Cobble
Steven Delopoulos
Christena Graves
Sara Groves
Maeve
Sandra McCracken
Andrew Osenga
Jill Paquette
Kendall Payne
Andrew Peterson
Jill Phillips
Robbie Seay Band
Jami Smith
Waterdeep
Derek Webb
Matt Wertz
Seth Woods

A Final Word

These times of transition in which we find ourselves have been described in many ways. It is widely agreed that both our secular and religious cultures—from the most liberal to the most conservative—have been deeply affected by a mind-set labeled "modern," and we now are grappling with the appearance of a new cultural ethos often called "postmodern." This transition has many dimensions: philosophical, artistic, technological, social, moral, economic, political, and theological. It is no surprise that in times of transition like these, fresh attention needs to be paid to how we translate, study, understand, teach, apply, and proclaim the vital message of the Scriptures.

During this unique time in the life of the church of Christ, there seems to be a change as to how we as the body of believers worship, fellowship, and communicate the truths of the gospel. ***The Voice*** appears at the point of impact where the modern church, with its tradition and stability, collides with the developing church of the future. We are working to help the church move through these changes and to focus its attention on God's Word. In reality, ***The Voice*** is the product of a community of believers seeking to bring alive the story of the Bible. The goal is to reinvigorate followers of Christ with the Scriptures. We are weaving together our talents to retell the story and create tools to use with the narrative communication of the Bible. Together we are rediscovering the story of the Bible.

The Voice of Matthew

It really is fitting that Matthew's Gospel is the first book in the New Testament, because it was after all the favorite Gospel of the early church for several reasons. You see the first disciples were all Jews, and Matthew sought to prove beyond a shadow of doubt that Jesus was the royal Messiah, the Son of David, the one chosen by God to rule over the Kingdom. So Matthew, more than the other Gospel writers, found Jesus' messiahship in strange and wonderful places where only the Jews would know to look. For example, Matthew prefaces his Gospel with a genealogy that begins with the announcement that Jesus is the Son of David (a messianic title). He then carefully traces Jesus' family line through David and concludes his genealogy of Jesus by pointing out that Jesus' family line could be divided neatly into three groups of 14 ancestors. Not coincidentally, David's name in Hebrew yields the number 14. For Matthew, Jesus' family line suggested that He was the Son of David, the Messiah; it was even in the numbers for the wise and understanding to see. Likewise, Matthew discovers Jesus' messianic role hidden cryptically in the name of His hometown Nazareth. Jesus and His family, we're told, settled in Nazareth to fulfill the prophecies, such as Isaiah 11:1 that calls Messiah—Branch. The word "branch" in Hebrew comes from the same root (*nzr)* as the word "Nazareth" (*nzrt*). When Matthew wrote his account of Jesus' life, he wanted his Jewish readers to contemplate the mystery, the correspondence between the oracle about the "Branch of David" prophesied in Isaiah and the village in Galilee where the holy family settled.

Jesus fulfilled Scripture in more ways than one. For example, Mary gives birth to Jesus in Bethlehem fulfilling the prophecy of Micah (5:2). According to Matthew, Joseph takes his family and flees to Egypt, to return after Herod's death. This fulfills the prophecy of Hosea 11:1, "out of Egypt I have called my son." Matthew wants his audience to consider how Jesus identified with the story of Israel—for a time even in exile in Egypt—and yet, unlike Israel, He did not fall into disobedience. According to Matthew, Jesus has come to fill the Scripture full by His teachings and His example. In this way, Jesus is a new Moses, a new Lawgiver. But again, He is the opposite of Moses because He doesn't receive the Law and write it on tablets of stone. He gives the Law and writes it directly on the hearts of His disciples and any who care to overhear the message of the kingdom of heaven.

Matthew intentionally structures his Gospel around five sermons of Jesus. For the evangelist's Jewish audience, the number five symbolized Torah, the first five books in the Bible. According to Matthew, the five sermons of Jesus complete the picture of Jesus as Lawgiver. They don't replace the five books of Torah, but his words refine and complement God's instruction to the people of the new covenant. Here are the five sermons that form the structure to the first Gospel:

Matthew 5-7 ....Sermon on the Mount
Matthew 10 ....Instructions for disciples on mission
Matthew 13 ....Parables of the Kingdom of Heaven
Matthew 18 ....Authentic Discipleship
Matthew 24-25 .....Sermon on the Last Days

When Jesus taught, the crowds were amazed at His teaching. Unlike other teachers in their day who taught with a borrowed authority, Jesus astounded the crowds and His opponents with His own authority. He even had the audacity to claim that His own authority matched that of the Scriptures. Wasn't it enough for Matthew that Jesus is the Messiah, the Son of David, the fulfillment of Scripture, the true Israel, the new Moses, and the new Lawgiver? No, there was more.

Matthew framed his entire story about Jesus with an *inclusio*, a literary device that works like bookends. The first bookend is located in Matthew 1:22-23. The true identity of the one born of a virgin is found in the prophetic name "Emmanuel"; Jesus is "God with us." The last bookend is found in Matthew 28:19-20 in what is commonly called the Great Commission. The commission ends with this promise: "I will be with you, day after day." Matthew wanted his audience, including us today, to read the entire story of Jesus against these two bookends. For Matthew, Jesus is more than the Messiah, the fulfiller of prophecies, the true son of Abraham, and the new Moses who brings a new Law, He is "God with us" who will be with us forever. That means that Jesus is no mere mortal; He is God in the flesh who comes to save us from our sins. For Matthew, the coming of Jesus into the world fulfills God's earlier promises to enter into our world to bring about redemption and a new creation (see particularly Isaiah 40—66). These images of Jesus that Matthew paints so beautifully fired the imaginations of Christians for centuries so that today, when we open our New Testaments, we find Matthew first in line.

From first word to last, no author is named or mentioned in the book. Unlike Paul's letters where the apostle's name sits prominently as the first word in the letter, all the Gospels are anonymous. But around A.D. 125, when the Gospels were gathered together, early Christians needed a way to distinguish one from the other. So they affixed the title "According to Matthew" to this Gospel because church traditions had credited this Gospel unanimously to Matthew, one of the twelve. Matthew 9:9-13 tells the story of how this tax collector gave up what was likely a lucrative tax collection agency to follow Jesus. Maybe that accounts for all his interest in the numbers.

— David Capes, PhD
Senior Theological and Biblical Reviewer
Ecclesia Bible Society

Matthew

THE GOSPEL ACCORDING TO

PROLOGUE

This is the story of Jesus the Son of David, Savior of the world, as recorded by Matthew, a disciple of our Lord. Now this account has been recorded for all those children of Abraham who have become followers of the true heir of the line of David so that they may know in whom they have believed. Because of our common Jewish heritage and living in the land of our fathers, we can understand Jesus of Nazareth—His miraculous healings, countless teachings filled with parables, righteous life, and lineage traced back to our father Abraham—as the One the prophets have spoken of since the early days.

This same Jesus is the Christ that we have been waiting for all these years. From the time when John the Teacher was ritually cleansing people in the Jordan, as a sign of rethinking their life of sin, to the wonderfully inspired teaching on the mountain in Galilee, throughout His parables, in His horrible death, and after His marvelous resurrection just days later, He is the King of the kingdom of heaven that He taught us about. There is no one like Jesus. The prophets of old looked for Him, David sang of Him, and our leaders feared Him. He is Messiah, King of kings, and husband of His new bride, the church.

We will begin with the lineage that establishes our Lord. Next we will examine His life, beginning with His birth and finishing with His resurrection. We will find that in His great teachings and in His exemplary life of holiness and service, Jesus is the great King we have anticipated.

Matthew

Chapter 1

THE LINEAGE OF JESUS

[1]This is the family history, the genealogy, of Jesus the Savior, *the*
coming King. You will see in this history that Jesus is descended from
King David, and that He is also descended from Abraham.

> Here is the actual lineage, the chain of fathers and sons that connects Abraham to David and David to Jesus:

[2]Abraham, *whom God called into a special, chosen, covenanted*
relationship, and who was the founding father of the nation of Israel,
was the father of Isaac; Isaac was the father of Jacob, Jacob was the
father of Judah, and of Judah's *11* brothers; [3]Judah was the father of
Perez and Zerah (and Perez and Zerah's mother was Tamar, *who*
was Judah's widowed daughter-in-law; she dressed up like a prostitute
and seduced her father-in-law, all so she could keep this very family
line alive); Perez was the father of Hezron; Hezron was the father of
Ram; [4]Ram was the father of Amminadab; Amminadab was the
father of Nahshon; Nahshon was the father of Salmon; [5]Salmon was
the father of Boaz (and Boaz's mother was Rahab, *a Canaanite pros-*
titute who heroically hid Israelite spies from hostile authorities who
wanted to kill them); Boaz was the father of Obed (his mother was
Ruth, *a Moabite woman who converted to the Hebrew faith*); Obed
was the father of Jesse; [6]And Jesse was the father of David, who was
the king *of the nation of Israel*. David was the father of Solomon (*his*
mother was Bathsheba, she was married to a man named Uriah);

> Solomon's mother was Bathsheba, the wife of Uriah, a soldier in David's army. She was bathing in her courtyard one evening, when David spied her and became interested in her. Later, Bathsheba got pregnant during an adulterous liaison with David, so David had Uriah killed in battle and then married his widow. David and Bathsheba's first baby died, but later Bathsheba got pregnant again and gave birth to Solomon.

[7]Solomon was the father of Rehoboam; Rehoboam was the father
of Abijah; Abijah was the father of Asa; [8]Asa was the father of
Jehoshaphat; Jehoshaphat was the father of Joram; Joram was the
father of Uzziah; [9]Uzziah was the father of Jotham; Jotham was the
father of Ahaz; Ahaz was the father of Hezekiah; [10]Hezekiah was the
father of Manasseh; Manasseh was the father of Amon; Amon was
the father of Josiah; [11]Josiah was the father of Jeconiah and his
brothers, and Josiah's family lived at the time *when God's chosen
people of Israel* were deported *from the promised land to* Babylon.

[12]After the deportation to Babylon, Jeconiah had a son, Shealtiel.
Shealtiel was the father of Zerubbabel, [13]Zerubbabel was the father
of Abiud; Abiud was the father of Eliakim; Eliakim was the father of
Azor; [14]Azor was the father of Zadok; Zadok was the father of
Achim; Achim was the father of Eliud; [15]Eliud was the father of
Eleazar; Eleazar was the father of Matthan; Matthan was the father
of Jacob; [16]Jacob was the father of Joseph, who married a woman
named Mary. It was Mary who gave birth to Jesus, and it is Jesus
who is *the Savior, the Anointed One*, the Messiah, the Christ.

[17]Abraham and David were linked with 14 generations, 14 generations link David to the Babylonian exile, and 14 more take us from the exile to the birth of Christ.

I've told you this long genealogy for a good reason: to show you how this Jesus fulfills the prophecies that tell us the Messiah will be a descendant of Abraham and of David.

And I've told you about some of the women in Jesus' line so you'll know God is gracious to everyone, even to prostitutes and adulterers. Because many of the women I listed weren't Israelites, but were strangers and foreigners, they foreshadow all the foreigners God will adopt into His church through Jesus. I've told you about these women so you know that the children in God's family are often conceived under strange circumstances (like Tamar's twins being conceived as she played the harlot, and like King Solomon being born to adulterous parents). Now that you know about this unusual family, you won't be surprised at what happens next—because what happens next is the conception of a baby under very strange circumstances.

18 So here, *finally*, is the story of the Messiah's birth *(it is quite a*
remarkable story): Mary was engaged to marry Joseph *son of David.*
They hadn't married. And yet, some time well before their wedding
date, Mary learned that she was pregnant by the Holy Spirit.
19 Joseph, because he was kind and upstanding and honorable, wanted to spare Mary shame. He did not wish to cause her more embar-
rassment than necessary.

This was remarkable, because Mary had never had sex. She and Joseph had not even spent very much time alone, but they were pledged to each other and their wedding feast was planned.

She had never even kissed a man. She was a virgin, yet she was pregnant. Miraculous! On the other hand, Joseph suspected that Mary had cheated on him and had sex with another man. He knew he would have to break their engagement, but he decided to break their engagement quietly. Mary understood that it was God, in the Person of the Holy Spirit, who had made her pregnant.

[20]Now when Joseph had decided to act on his instincts, an angel of the Lord came to him in a dream.

Angel of the Lord Joseph, son of David, do not be afraid to wed Mary and *bring her into your home and family* as your wife. *She did not sneak off and sleep with someone else*—rather, she conceived the baby she now carries through the miraculous wonderworking of the Holy Spirit. [21]She will have a Son, and you will name Him Jesus, which means *"the Lord Saves,"* because this Jesus is the Person who will save all of His people from sin.

[24]Joseph woke up from his dream and did exactly what the angel had told him to do: he married Mary and brought her into his home as his wife [25](though he did not consummate their marriage until after her Son was born). *And when the baby was born,* Joseph named him Jesus, *Savior.**

[22]*This is a remarkable and strange story. But it is not wholly surprising because years and years ago, Isaiah,* a prophet of Israel, foretold the story of Mary, Joseph, and Jesus.

Isaiah [23]A virgin will conceive and bear a Son, and His name will be Emmanuel (which is a Hebrew name that means "God with us").*

1:25 Verses 24 and 25 have been moved before verse 22 to help the reader understand the continuity of the passage.
1:23 Isaiah 7:14

Mary and Joseph named their baby Jesus, but sometimes we refer to Him as Emmanuel, because by coming to dwell with us, living and dying among us, He was able to save us from our sin.

CHAPTER 2

THE BABY SAVIOR

[1]Jesus was born in the town of Bethlehem, in the province of Judea,
at the time when King Herod reigned. *Not long after Jesus was born,*
magi, wise men or seers from the East, *understood that the One who*
would save His people from sin had been born, so they set off to find
the baby Savior. Making their way from the East to Jerusalem, these
wise men asked, [2]"Where is this newborn, who is the King of the
Jews? When we were far away in the East we saw His star, and we
have followed its glisten and gleam all this way to worship Him."

[3]King Herod began to hear rumors of the wise men's quest, and
he, and all of his followers in Jerusalem, were worried. [4]So Herod
called all of the leading Jewish teachers, the chief priests and head
scribes, and he asked them where *Hebrew tradition claimed* the
long-awaited Savior would be born.

Scribes and Priests | [5]*An ancient Hebrew prophet, Micah,* said this: [6]"'But
you, Bethlehem, in the land of Judah, are no poor
relation—for from your people will come a Ruler
who will be the shepherd of My people Israel.'"*

From that prophecy we learn that the Savior would be born in the town of Bethlehem, in the province of Judea. This information in hand, Herod ordered the wise men to come to his chambers in secret, and when they arrived, Herod quizzed them.

2:6 Micah 5:2

[7]Herod called the wise men to him, demanding to know the exact time the special star had appeared to them. [8]Then Herod sent them to Bethlehem.

Herod | Go *to Bethlehem* and search high and low for this *Savior* child, and as soon as you know where He is, report it to me, so I may go and worship Him.

> Herod, of course, didn't really want to worship the baby Jesus. He wanted to kill Him. He was being crafty, trying to trick the magi into betraying the One they sought. But it didn't work.

[9-10]The wise men *left Herod's chambers* and went on their way. The star they had first seen in the East reappeared—a miracle that, of course, overjoyed and enraptured the wise men. The star led them to the house where Jesus lay, [11]and as soon as the wise men arrived, they saw Him with His mother Mary, and they bowed down and worshiped Him. They unpacked their satchels and gave Jesus gifts of gold, frankincense, and myrrh.

> These were exceptionally good gifts, for gold is what you give a king, and Jesus is the King of kings; incense is what you give a priest, and Jesus is the High Priest of all high priests; myrrh ointment is used to heal, and Jesus is a healer. But myrrh is also used to embalm corpses—and Jesus was born to die.

[12]And then, *just as Joseph did a few months before*, the wise men had a dream warning them not to go back to Herod. *The wise men heeded the dream. Ignoring Herod's instructions*, they returned to their homes in the East by a different route.

[13]After the wise men left, an angel of the Lord appeared to Joseph in a dream.

As you can see, God does at times speak to His people through dreams.

Angel *(to Joseph)* | Get up, take the Child and His mother, and head to Egypt. Stay there until I tell you *it is safe to leave.* For Herod *understands that Jesus threatens him and all he stands for.* He is planning to search for the Child and kill Him. *But you will be safe in Egypt.*

[14]So Joseph got up in the middle of the night; he bundled up Mary and Jesus, and they left for Egypt.*

[16]*After a few months had passed,* Herod realized he'd been tricked. The wise men *were not coming back; they weren't going to lead him to the infant King.* Herod, *of course,* was furious, *but he was not to be outdone.* He simply ordered that all boys who lived in or near Bethlehem and were two years of age and younger be killed. *He knew the baby King was this age* because of what the wise men told him.

Herod knew ordinary babies would die in this purge, but he didn't care—Herod was not so much cold-blooded as pragmatic, willing to do whatever was necessary to kill this new supposed King. And so all those other baby boys died. But, of course, Herod's plan ultimately failed. He didn't know the baby Savior had been whisked to safety in Egypt.

2:14 Verse 15 has been moved to follow verse 18 to help the reader understand the continuity of the passage.

[17]This *sad event* had long been foretold by the prophet Jeremiah:

Jeremiah | [18]A voice will be heard in Ramah, weeping *and wailing* and mourning *out loud all day and night.* The voice is Rachel's, weeping for her children, her children who have been killed; she weeps, and she will not be comforted.*

[15]Joseph, Mary, and Jesus *stayed in Egypt* until Herod died. This fulfilled yet another prophecy. The prophet *Hosea* once wrote, "Out of Egypt I called My Son."*

[19]And after Herod died, an angel of the Lord appeared in a dream to Joseph in Egypt:

Angel of the Lord | [20]*You may go home now.* Take the Child and His mother and go back to the land of Israel, for the people who were trying to take the Child's life are now dead.

[21]So Joseph got up and took Mary and Jesus and returned to the
land of Israel. [22]Soon he learned that Archelaus, Herod's *oldest and notoriously brutal* son, was ruling Judea. *Archelaus, Joseph knew, might not be any friendlier to Joseph and his family than Herod had been.* Joseph was simply afraid. *He had another dream, and* in this dream, he was warned *away from Judea*; so Joseph *decided* to settle *up north in a district called* Galilee,
[23]in a town called Nazareth. And this, too, fulfilled what the prophets have taught, "*The Savior* will be a Nazarene."*

2:18 Jeremiah 31:15
2:15 Hosea 11:1
2:23 Judges 13:5; Isaiah 11:1

Nazarene, as you may know, means, "tender branch, green branch, the branch that is living." And that, of course, is what this Jesus is. He is the living Branch, the branch of David that extends the reach of the tree of Israel, eventually to the Gentiles.

CHAPTER 3

A MAN CALLED JOHN

[1]Around the same time, a man called John* began to travel, preach, and ritually wash people in the wilderness of Judea. *John preached a stern but exciting message.*

John | [2]Repent! For the kingdom of heaven is near.

[3]John's proclamation fulfilled a promise made by the *ancient* prophet Isaiah, who had said, "There will be a voice calling from the desert, saying,

'Prepare the road for God's journey;
in the desert *repair* and straighten out every *mile* of God's highway.'"*

[4]John *was all about wilderness. He preached in the wilderness. He wore wild* clothes made from camel hair with a leather belt around his waist—the clothes of an outcast, a rebel—*clothes just like the prophet Elijah had worn.* He ate locusts and wild honey.

> Sometimes when people saw John they were reminded of the last time God's people had wandered in a wilderness—after the exodus from Egypt. They thought perhaps John was inaugurating a new

3:1 Literally, John who immersed, to show repentance
3:3 Isaiah 40:3

exodus. (Actually, that is a pretty good way to think of it. The Messiah, whose way John came to prepare, would call us away from comfort and status; He would call us all to challenge our assumptions and the things we take for granted.)

5People from Jerusalem, all of Judea, and indeed from all around the
river Jordan came to John. 6They confessed their sins, and they
were dunked* by him in the Jordan.

7*But John was—well, he was not exactly warm to all those who
came to him seeking cleansing.** He told some Pharisees and
Sadducees who came for the ritual,

John | *You children of serpents!* You brood of vipers! Did
someone suggest you flee from the wrath that is
upon us? 8-9 *If you think that simply hopping in the
Jordan will cleanse you, then you are sorely mistaken.* Your life must bear the fruits of turning toward righteousness. Nor are you correct if you think that being descended from Abraham is enough to make you holy and right with God. *Yes, the children of Abraham are God's chosen children,* but God can adopt as daughters and sons anyone He likes—*He can turn these stones into sons if He likes.*

To be made right with God, you must truly repent. Living for God must overtake your whole life, your whole being. Don't you know what repent means? It means to turn completely away from sin, and completely toward God.

3:6 Literally, immerse, to show repentance
3:7 Literally, immersion, an act of repentance

John [10]Even now, there is an ax poised at the root of every tree, and every tree that does not bear good fruit will be cut down and tossed into the fire. [11]I ritually cleanse* you as a mark of turning your life around. But someone is coming after me, someone whose sandals I am not fit to carry, someone who is more powerful than I. He will wash* you *not in water*, but in fire and with the Holy Spirit. [12]He carries a winnowing fork in His hand, and He will clear His threshing floor; He will gather up the good wheat in His barn, and He will burn the chaff with a fire that cannot be put out.

[13]And then, *the One of whom John spoke—the all-powerful One, the One who carried that winnowing fork—that One, of course, was* Jesus—He came to the Jordan from Galilee to be washed* by John. [14]At first, John demurred.

John I need to be cleansed* by You. Why do You come to me?

Jesus [15]It will be right, true, and faithful to God's chosen path for you to cleanse Me *with your hands in the Jordan River*.

John agreed, and he ritually cleansed Jesus, dousing Him in the waters of the Jordan. [16] Jesus emerged* from the water, and at that moment

---

3:11 Literally, immerse, to show repentance
3:11 Literally, immerse, in a rite of initiation and purification
3:13 Literally, immerse, to show repentance
3:14 Literally, immerse, in a rite of initiation and purification
3:16 Literally, when immersed, to show repentance

heaven was opened, and Jesus saw the Spirit of God descending like a dove and coming upon Him, *alighting on His very body*.

A Voice from Heaven

[17]This is My Son, whom I love; *this is the Apple of My eye*; with Him I am well pleased.

CHAPTER 4

JESUS AND THE DEVIL

1The Spirit then led Jesus into the desert to be tempted by the devil.
2Jesus fasted for 40 days and 40 nights. After this fast, He was, *as
you can imagine*, hungry. 3*But He was also curiously stronger because
of His fast. And so He was able to withstand the devil, the tempter,
when he came to Jesus.*

The Devil	If You are the Son of God, tell these stones to become bread.
Jesus *(quoting Deuteronomy)*	4It is written, "Man does not live by bread alone. Rather, he lives on every word that comes from the mouth of God."*

> The point, of course, is not that Jesus couldn't have turned these stones to bread. As you will see a little later in our story, He can make food appear when He needs to. But Jesus doesn't work miracles out of the blue, for no reason, for show or proof or spectacle. He works them in intimate, close places; He works them to meet people's needs and to show them the way to the Kingdom.

5Then the devil took Jesus to the holy city, *Jerusalem,* and he had
Jesus stand at the very highest point in the holy temple.

4:4 Deuteronomy 8:3

The Devil | [6]If You are the Son of God, jump! *And then we will see if You fulfill* the Scripture that says, "He will command His angels concerning You, and the angels will buoy You in their hands, so that *You will not crash, or fall, or even* graze Your foot on a stone."*

Jesus | [7]That is not the only thing Scripture says. It also says, "Do not put the LORD your God to the test."*

[8]And still the devil *subjected Jesus to a third test. He* took Jesus to the top of a very high mountain, and he showed Jesus all the kingdoms of the world in all their *splendor and* glory, *their power and pomp.*

The Devil | [9]If You bow down and worship me, I will give You all these kingdoms.

Jesus | [10]Get away from Me, Satan. *I will not serve you. I will instead follow* Scripture, which tells us to "worship the LORD your God, and serve only Him."*

[11]Then, the devil left Jesus. And angels came and ministered to
Him.
[12]*It was not long until powerful people put* John in prison. When
Jesus learned this, He went back to Galilee. [13]He moved from
Nazareth to Capernaum, a town by the sea in the regions of Zebulun
and Naphtali—[14]He did this to fulfill one of the prophecies of Isaiah:

4:6 Psalm 91:11-12
4:7 Deuteronomy 6:16
4:10 Deuteronomy 6:13

15“In the land of Zebulun and the land of Naphtali, the road to the
sea along the Jordan in Galilee, the land of the Gentiles—16*in these
places*, the people who had been living in darkness saw a great light.
The light of life will overtake those who dwelt in the shadowy darkness of death.”*

17From that time on, preaching was part of Jesus’ work. *His message was not dissimilar from John’s.*

Jesus | *Turn away from sin; turn toward God.* Repent, for the kingdom of heaven is at hand.

By now Jesus desired a community around Him, friends and followers who would help Him carry this urgent, precious message to people. And so He called a community around Him. We call these first beloved followers *disciples,* which means "apprentices." The first disciples were two brothers, Simon and Andrew. They were fishermen.

18*One day* Jesus was walking along the Sea of Galilee when He
saw Simon (also called Peter) and Andrew throwing their nets into
the water. They were, of course, fishermen.

Jesus | 19*Come,* follow Me, and I will make you fishers of
men.

20Immediately, Peter and Andrew left their fishnets and followed
Jesus.

21Going on from there, Jesus saw two more brothers, James the
son of Zebedee and his brother John. *They, too, were fishermen.*
They were in a boat with their father Zebedee getting their nets
ready to fish. Jesus summoned them, *just as He had called to Peter*

4:16 Isaiah 9:1-2

and Andrew, [22]and immediately they left their boat and their father to follow Jesus.

[23]And so Jesus went throughout Galilee. He taught in the synagogues. He preached the good news of the Kingdom, and He healed people, ridding their bodies of sickness and disease. [24]*People talked about this Jesus, this Preacher and Healer,* and word *of His charisma and wisdom and power and love* spread all over Syria, as more and more sick people came to Him. *People who were too sick to walk persuaded their friends and relatives to carry them to Jesus.* The innumerable ill who came before Him had all sorts of diseases—they were in crippling pain; they were possessed by demons; they had seizures; they were paralyzed. But Jesus healed them *all.* [25]Large crowds from Galilee, from Jerusalem, from *the ten cities called* the Decapolis, from Judea, and from the region across the Jordan—*these cripples and demonized and ill and paralytics came to Jesus, and He healed them, and they followed Him.*

CHAPTER 5

FULFILLING THE SACRED LAW

1 Now when He saw the crowds, He went up on a mountain *(as
Moses had done before Him)* and He sat down *(as Jewish teachers of
His day usually did)*. His disciples gathered around Him.

> There on the mountain Jesus taught them all. And as He was teaching, crowds crowded around and overheard His teachings, listened in, and were captivated, just as you who now hear this story or sit with this book in your hand are invited to come around and listen in and hear and be taught and be captivated.

And He began to teach them.

Jesus

3 Blessed are the spiritually poor—the kingdom of
heaven is theirs.
4 Blessed are those who mourn, *who weep about sin
and long for how things are supposed to be*—they
will be comforted.
5 Blessed are the *meek and* gentle—they will inherit
the earth.
6 Blessed are those who hunger and thirst for
righteousness—they will be filled.
7 Blessed are the merciful—they will be shown mercy.
8 Blessed are those who are pure in heart—they will
see God.

9Blessed are the peacemakers—they will be called
children of God.
10Blessed are those who are persecuted because of
righteousness—the kingdom of heaven is theirs.
11And blessed are you, *blessed are all of you,* when
people persecute you or denigrate you or
despise you or tell lies about you on My
account. 12*But when this happens,* rejoice. Be
glad. Remember that God's prophets have been
persecuted in the past. And know that in
heaven, you have a great reward.

And be sure, you will be despised because of Jesus. You will be persecuted and tarred and targeted and tarnished and cursed because you have loved and followed Him.

And Jesus continued by teaching about salt. Just as salt draws out the good flavors subtly hidden in our food, you help creation be its truest self. As salt preserves food that would otherwise spoil, you help preserve the goodness of creation. So, too, those who claim to be children of God, but live selfish, small lives, have no part in the kingdom of heaven. They will be thrown out and trampled.

Jesus 13You, *beloved,* are the salt of the earth. But if salt
becomes bland and loses its saltiness, can anything
make it salty again? *No.* It is useless. *It just lies
there, white and bland and grainy.* It is tossed out,
thrown away, or trampled.
14And you, *beloved,* are the light of the world. A
city built on a hilltop cannot be hidden. 15Similarly,
it would be silly to light a lamp and then hide it
under a bowl. When someone lights a lamp, she

puts it on a table or a desk or a chair, and the light
illumines the entire house. [16]*You are like that illu-*
minating light. Let your light shine everywhere you
go, *that you may illumine creation,* so men and
women everywhere may see your good actions,
may see *creation at its fullest, may see your devo-*
tion to Me, and may turn and praise your Father in
heaven *because of it.*

[17]Do not think that I have come to overturn or do
away with the law or the words of our prophets. *To*
the contrary: I have not come to overturn them but
to fulfill them. *I ask you not merely to follow the*
Commandments, but to give Me your heart, your
body, and your very life.

[18]This, *beloved,* is the truth: until heaven and
earth disappear, not one letter, not one pen stroke,
will disappear from sacred Law—for everything,
everything in the sacred Law will be fulfilled and
accomplished. *Our community is not about destroy-*
ing the Law. [19]Anyone who breaks even the small-
est, most obscure commandment—not to mention
teaches others to do the same—will be called small
and obscure in the kingdom of heaven. Those who
practice the Law and teach others how to live the
Law will be called great in the kingdom of heaven.
[20]For I tell you this: you will not enter the kingdom
of heaven unless your righteousness goes deeper
than the Pharisees, even more righteous than the
most learned learner of the Law. *And this is one*
reason I have come to you, beloved—to make you
righteous, through and through.

*[21]And then Jesus began to interpret the Law of Scripture for the
people:*

Jesus | As you know, long ago God instructed *Moses to tell*
His people, "Do not murder; those who murder will
be judged *and punished.*"* [22]*But here is the even
harder truth*: anyone who is angry with his brother
will be judged for his anger. Anyone who *taunts his
friend, speaks contemptuously toward him, or* calls
him "Loser" or "Fool" or "Scum," will have to
answer to the high court. And anyone who calls his
brother a fool may find himself in the fires of hell.

[23]Therefore, if you are bringing an offering to
God, and you remember that your brother is angry
at you or holds a grudge against you, [24]then leave
your gift before the altar, go to your brother, *repent,
and forgive one another*, be reconciled, and then
return to the altar to offer your gift to God. *It does
not matter if it took you three days to get to the temple—go home and reconcile with your brother before
you make your offering to God.*

[25]If someone sues you, settle things with him
quickly. Talk to him as you are walking to court—
otherwise, he may turn matters over to the judge,
and the judge may turn you over to an officer, and
you may land in jail. [26]I tell you this: you will not
emerge from prison until you have paid your last
penny.

[27]As you know, long ago God forbade His people
to commit adultery.* [28]*You may think you have abid-*

5:21 Exodus 20:13
5:27 Exodus 20:14

ed by this Commandment, walked the straight and
narrow, but I tell you this: any man who looks at a
woman with lust has already committed adultery
in his heart. [29]If your right eye leads you into sin,
gouge it out and throw it *in the garbage*—for better
you lose one part of your body than march your
entire body *through the gates of sin and* into hell.
[30]And if your right hand leads you into sin, cut it off
and throw it away—for better you lose one part of
your body than march your entire body *through the*
gates of sin and into hell.

[31]And here is something else: *you have read in*
Deuteronomy that anyone who divorces his wife
must do so fairly—he must give her the requisite
certificate of divorce *and send her on her way, free*
*and unfettered.** [32]But I tell you this: unless your
wife cheats on you, you must not divorce her, peri-
od. Nor are you to marry someone who has been
married and divorces, for a divorced person who
remarries commits adultery.

[33]You know that God expects us to abide by the
oaths we swear and the promises we make. [34]But I
tell you this: do not ever swear an oath. *What is an*
oath? You cannot say, "I swear by heaven"—*for*
heaven is not yours to swear by; it is God's throne.
[35]And you cannot say, "I swear by this good earth,"
for the earth is not yours to swear by; it is God's
footstool. And you cannot say, "I swear by the holy
city Jerusalem," for *it is not yours to swear by; it is*
the city *of God, the capital* of the King of kings.
[36]You cannot even say that you swear by your own

5:31 Deuteronomy 24:1

head, *for God has dominion over your hands, your*
lips, your head. It is He who determines if your hair
be *straight or curly,* white or black; *it is He who*
rules over even this small scrap of creation, one lock
of straight hair, one cutting of curls. [37]*You need not*
swear an oath—any impulse to do so is of evil.
Simply let your "yes" be "yes," and let your "no" be
"no."

[38]You know that *Hebrew Scripture* sets this standard *of justice and punishment*: take an eye for an
eye and a tooth for a tooth.* [39]But I say this, don't
fight against the one who is working evil against
you: *do not gouge the eye of one who gouges your*
eye, and do not crush the tooth of one who makes
you toothless. If someone strikes you on the right
cheek, you are to turn and offer him your left
cheek. [40]If someone connives to get your shirt, give
him your jacket as well. [41]If someone forces you to
walk with him for a mile, walk with him for two
instead. [42]If someone asks you for something, give
it to him. If someone wants to borrow something
from you, do not turn away.

[43]You have been taught to love your neighbor
and hate your enemy.* [44]But I tell you this: love
your enemies. Pray for those who torment you and
persecute you—[45]in so doing, you become children
of your Father in heaven. *He, after all, loves each of*
us—good and evil, kind and cruel. He causes the sun
to rise *and shine* on evil and good alike. He causes
the rain *to water the fields* of the righteous and *the*

5:38 Exodus 21:24; Leviticus 24:20; Deuteronomy 19:21
5:43 Leviticus 19:18

fields of the sinner. 46It is easy to love those who
love you—even a tax collector can love those who
love him. 47And it is easy to greet your friends—
even Gentiles do that! 48*But you are called to something higher:* "Be perfect, as your Father in heaven
is perfect."

CHAPTER 6

DON'T WORRY

Jesus | 1*Part of imitating the perfection of God is acting
charitably and generously, doing good deeds, work-
ing for justice, and praying. But when you do these
righteous acts, *do not do them in front of spectators.*
Don't do them where you can be seen, *let alone*
lauded, by others. If you do, you will have no
reward from your Father in heaven. 2When you
give to the poor, *do not boast about it*, announcing
your donations with blaring trumpets as the play
actors do. Do not brazenly give your charity in the
synagogues and on the streets; *indeed, do not give*
at all if you are giving because you want to be
praised by your neighbors. Those people who give
in order to reap praise have already received their
reward. 3-4When you give to the needy, do it in
secret—even your left hand should not know what
your right hand is doing. Then your Father, who
sees in secret, will reward you.

5Likewise, when you pray, do not be hypocrites
who love to pray loudly at synagogue or on street
corners—their concern is *not meant to be heard by*
God (who can hear even the softest of whispers) but
to be seen by men. *Those people who sing their*
prayers with bravado and show, so that their neigh-
bors might see them and be impressed with their

piety—they have already earned their reward.
6 When you pray, go into a private room, close the
door, and pray unseen to your Father who is
unseen. Then your Father, who sees in secret, will
reward you.

7 And when you pray do not go on and on, exces-
sively and strangely like the Gentiles—they think
their verbosity will *let them be heard by their*
deities. 8 Do not be like them. *Your prayers need not*
be labored or lengthy or grandiose—for your Father
knows what you need before you ever ask Him.

9 Your prayers, *rather*, should be *simple*, like this:

Our Father in heaven,
    let Your name remain holy.
10 Bring about Your kingdom.
Manifest Your will here on earth,
    as it is manifest in heaven.
11 Give us each day that day's bread, *no more,*
    no less,
12 And forgive us our debts,
    as we forgive those who owe us something.
13 Lead us not into temptation,
    but deliver us from evil.
[But let Your kingdom be,
    and let it be powerful
    and glorious forever. Amen.]*

You will notice that in this prayer, you are told to declare your forgiveness of those who have wronged you—you forgive them their sins, and you forgive them their debts. This is because your forgiveness of other people emulates God's forgiveness of you.

6:13 The last part of verse 13 is omitted by some of the earliest manuscripts.

Jesus [14]If you forgive people when they sin against you,
then your Father will forgive you *when you sin*
against Him and when you sin against your neigh-
bor. [15]But if you do not forgive your neighbors' sins,
your Father will not forgive your sins.

[16]And when you fast, do not look miserable as *the*
actors and hypocrites do when they are fasting—
they walk around town putting on airs about their
suffering and weakness, complaining about how
hungry they are. So everyone will know they are
fasting, they don't wash or anoint themselves with
oil, *pink their cheeks, or wear comfortable shoes.*
Those who show off their piety, they have already
received their reward. [17]When you fast, wash your
face and beautify yourself with oil, [18]so no one who
looks at you will know about your discipline. Only
your Father, who is unseen, will see your fast. And
your Father, who sees in secret, will reward you.

[19]Some people store up treasures *in their homes*
here on earth. *This is a shortsighted practice*—don't
undertake it. Moths and rust will eat up any treasure you may store here. Thieves may break into
your homes and steal *your precious trinkets.*
[20]Instead, put up your treasures in heaven where
moths do not attack, where rust does not corrode,
and where thieves are barred at the door. [21]For
where your treasure is, there your heart will be
also.

[22]The eye is the lamp of the body. *You draw light*
into your body through your eyes, and light shines
out to the world through your eyes. So if your eye is
well *and shows you what is true,* then your whole

body will be filled with light. [23]But if your eye is
clouded *or evil,* then your body will be filled with
evil and dark clouds. And the darkness that takes
over the body *of a child of God who has gone*
astray—that is the deepest, darkest darkness
there is.

When Jesus speaks of eyes and light, He means keep your eyes on God for your eyes are the windows of your soul. And do not look at trash—at pornography, at filth, at expensive baubles you will soon lust after. And this is what He means when He says, "Where your treasure is, there your heart will be also": where your eyes are, there your treasure will be.

Jesus [24]No one can serve two masters. *If you try,* you will
wind up loving the first master and hating the second, or vice versa. People try to serve both God
and money—but you can't. *You must choose one or*
the other.

[25]Here is the bottom line: do not worry about
your life. Don't worry about what you will eat or
what you will drink. Don't worry about how you
clothe your body. Living is about more than merely
eating, and the body is about more than dressing
up. [26]Look at the birds in the sky. *They do not store*
food for winter. They don't plant gardens. They do
not sow or reap—and yet, they are always fed
because your heavenly Father feeds them. And you
are even more precious to Him than a beautiful
bird. *If He looks after them, of course He will look*
after you. [27]*Worrying does not do any good*—who

here can claim to add even an hour to his life by
worrying?
[28]Nor should you worry about clothes. Consider
the lilies of the field and how they grow. They do
not work or weave or sew, *and yet their garments*
are stunning. [29]Even King Solomon, dressed in his
most regal garb, was not as lovely as these lilies.
[30]*And think about grassy fields*—the grasses are here
now, but they will be dead by winter. And yet God
adorns them so radiantly. How much more will He
clothe you, you of little faith, *you who have no*
trust?
[31]So do not consume yourself with questions:
What will we eat? What will we drink? What will
we wear? [32]Gentiles make themselves frantic over
such questions—*they don't realize that* your heavenly Father knows exactly what you need. [33]Seek
first the kingdom of God and His righteousness,
and then all these things will be given to you, *too.*
[34]So do not worry about tomorrow. Let tomorrow
worry about itself. Living faithfully is a large
enough task for today.

CHAPTER 7

DON'T JUDGE

Jesus [1]If you judge *other people*, then you will find that you, too, are being judged. [2]Indeed, you will be judged by the very standards to which you hold other people.

So when you are tempted to criticize your neighbor because her house isn't clean enough, she seems ill-tempered, or a bit flighty—remember those same standards and judgments will come back to you. Don't criticize your neighbor for being short-tempered one morning, when you yourself are snippish and snappish and waspish all the time.

Jesus [3]Why is it that you see the dust in your brother's or sister's eye, but you can't see what is in your own eye? [4]Don't ignore the wooden plank in your eye, but criticize the speck of sawdust in your brother's eyelashes. [5]That type of criticism and judgment is a sham! Remove the plank from your own eye, and then perhaps you will be able to see clearly how to help your brother flush out his sawdust.

[6]Don't give precious things to dogs. Don't cast your pearls before swine. If you do, the pigs will trample the pearls with their *little pigs'* feet, and then they will turn back and attack you.

When you have been given something valuable—whether it is a holy book, a family relic, or a valuable insight or teaching—don't waste it on someone who will just laugh at you.

Now Jesus returns to the topic of prayer. Prayer is so very important and sometimes so hard, but He helps us focus here by giving us the very essence of prayer:

Jesus [7]Just ask and it will be given to you; seek after it
and you will find. *Continue to* knock and the door
will be opened for you. [8]All who ask receive. Those
who seek, find what they seek. And he who
knocks, will have the door opened.

[9]Think of it this way: if your son asked you for
bread, would you give him a stone? *Of course not—*
you would give him a loaf of bread. [10]If your son
asked for a fish, would you give him a snake? *No, to*
be sure, you would give him a fish—the best fish you
could find. [11]So if you, who are sinful, know how to
give your children good gifts, how much more so
does your Father in heaven, who is perfect, know
how to give great gifts to His children!

[12]This is what our Scriptures come to teach: in
everything, in every circumstance, do to others as
you would have them do to you.

[13]*There are two paths before you; you may take*
only one path. One doorway is narrow. *And one*
door is wide. Go through the narrow door. For the
wide door leads to a wide path, and the wide path
is broad, and the wide, broad path is easy, and the
wide, broad, easy path has many, many people on

it, but the wide, broad, easy, crowded path leads to
death. 14Now then, that narrow door leads to a narrow road that in turn leads to life. It is hard to find
that road. Not many people manage it.

15Along the way, watch out for false prophets.
They will come to you in sheep's clothing, but
underneath *that quaint and innocent wool, they* are
hungry wolves. 16But you will recognize them by
their fruits. You don't find *sweet, delicious* grapes
growing on thorny bushes, do you? You don't find
delectable figs growing in the midst of *prickly* this-
tles. 17*People and communities and lives are like
trees.* Good trees bear beautiful, tasty fruit, but bad
trees bear ugly, bitter fruit. 18A good tree cannot
bear ugly, bitter fruit; nor can a bad tree bear fruit
that is beautiful and tasty. 19And what happens to
the rotten trees? They are cut down. They are used
for firewood. 20*When a prophet comes to you and
preaches this or that* look for his fruits: *sweet or
sour? rotten or ripe?*

21Not everyone who says to Me, "Lord, Lord,"
will enter the kingdom of heaven. *Simply calling
Me "Lord" when you reach heaven will not be
enough.* Only those who do the will of My Father
who is in heaven *will join Me in heaven.* 22*At the end
of time, on the day of judgment*—on that day, many
will say to Me "Lord, Lord, did we not prophesy in
Your name? Did we not drive demons out *of the
possessed* in Your name? Did we not perform miracles in Your name?" 23But I will say to them, "I
never knew you. And now, you must get away from
Me, you evildoers!"

> [24]Those people who are listening to Me, those people who *hear what I say and* live according to My teachings—you are like a wise man who built his house on a rock, *on a firm foundation.* [25]When storms hit, *rain pounded down* and waters rose, *levies broke* and winds beat all the walls of that house. But the house did not fall, because it was built upon rock. [26]Those of you who are listening and do not hear, *those who are listening and ignore My teachings, and those who take the wider, easier path, keeping company with false prophets:* you are like a fool who builds a house on sand. [27]When a storm comes to his house, *what will happen*? The rain will fall, the waters will rise, the wind will blow, and his house will collapse with a great crash. *Because it is built on nothing, on ephemera, on shifty, shifting sands.*

[28]With that Jesus finished His teaching, and the crowds were amazed by all He had said. [29]But Jesus taught in His own name, on His own authority, not like the scribes.

In some ways, He had taught like the rabbis of old; in other ways, this teaching was new and different. For usually rabbis cited other rabbis, generations of rabbis before them. He honored the Torah, but He was clear and insistent—this is the way we must read the Torah now.

CHAPTER 8

A LEPER, A CENTURION, A STORM, AND DEMONS

1 Large crowds followed Jesus when He came down from the mountain. 2 *And as Jesus was going along,* a leper approached Him and
knelt down before Him,

Leper: Lord, if You wish to, *please* heal me and make me clean!

Jesus *(stretching out His hand)*: 3 Of course I wish to. Be clean.

Immediately, the man was healed.

Jesus: 4 Don't tell anyone *what just happened.* Rather, go to the priest, show yourself to him, and give a wave offering as Moses commanded. Your actions will tell the story of what happened here today.

5 Eventually, Jesus came to *the little town of* Capernaum. In
Capernaum, a military officer came to Him and asked Him for help.

Officer: 6 Lord, I have a servant who is lying at home in agony, paralyzed.

Jesus: 7 I will come *to your house,* and I will heal him.

Officer | [8]Lord, I don't deserve to have You in my house.
And, in truth, I know You don't need to be with my
servant to heal him. Just say the word, and he will
be healed. [9]That, after all, is how authority works.
My troops obey me whether I am next to them or
not—*similarly, this sickness that is plaguing my ser-*
vant will obey You, whether You heal him from his
bedside or from across an ocean.

[10]Jesus was stunned by the depth of the officer's faith.

Jesus *(to His followers)* | This is the plain truth: I have not met a single
person in Israel with as much faith *as this officer*.
[11]It will not be just the children of Abraham and
Isaac and Jacob who celebrate at their heavenly
banquet at the end of time. No, people will come
from the East and the West—*and those who recog-*
nize Me, regardless of their lineage, will sit with Me
at that feast. [12]But those who have feigned their
faith will be cast out into outer darkness where
people weep and gnash their teeth.

[13]Then Jesus turned to the Centurion.

Jesus | You may go home, *and when you get home, you will see that your servant is just fine.* For it is as you say it is; it is as you believe.

And the officer's servant was healed, right then.

> What happened next seemed to embody the officer's wise opinion about authority: over and over Jesus showed just what His authority meant.

[14]Jesus went to Peter's house, and there He saw Peter's mother-in-
law lying in bed, sick and burning up with a fever. [15]Jesus touched
her hand, and *then she was healed*—the fever vanished. She got up
from bed and began to wait on Him.

[16]Toward nighttime, many people who were possessed by demons
were brought to Jesus, and He said one word of command and drove
the demons out, healing everyone who was sick. [17]These miraculous
healings fulfilled what the prophet Isaiah had predicted: "He took
our infirmities upon Himself, and He bore our diseases."*

[18]Jesus saw that a crowd had gathered around Him, and He told
the people to go to the other side *of the sea*. [19]A scribe came up to
Him.

Scribe Teacher, I will follow You wherever You go.

Jesus [20]Foxes have dens *in which to sleep*, and the birds have nests. But the Son of Man has no place to lay His head.

Disciple [21]Jesus, before I do the things You've asked me to do, I must first bury my father.

Jesus [22]Follow Me! And let the dead bury their own dead.

Did Jesus say, "Fair enough, you must of course bury your father. Just catch up with Me when you are done"? No. You see, this is one of the strange and radical things Jesus brought about—our families are no longer our families. Our deepest bonds are not those of blood. Our family now is found in the bonds of fellowship made possible by this Jesus.

8:17 Isaiah 53:4

23 And then Jesus got into a boat, and His disciples followed Him.
24 Out of nowhere, a vicious storm blew over the sea. Waves were
lapping up over the boat, threatening to overtake it! Yet Jesus was
asleep. 25 *Frightened (not to mention confused—how could anyone
sleep through this?),* the disciples woke Him up.

Disciples | Lord, save us! We're going to drown!

Jesus | 26 Please! What are you so afraid of, you of little faith?

And these, remember, were Jesus' close disciples! Jesus got up, told
the wind and the waves to calm down, and they did. The sea became
still and calm, *pacific once again.* 27 The disciples were astonished.
This Jesus was no ordinary miracle worker.

Disciples | Who is this? What sort of man is He, that the sea and the winds listen to Him?

28 Eventually Jesus came to the other side *of the sea,* to the region
of the Gadarenes. There, two men *who lived* near the tombs and
were possessed by demons came out *to the seaside and* met Jesus.
They were flailing about, so violent that they obstructed the path of
anyone who came their way.

Demons *(screaming at Jesus)* | 29 Why are You here? Have You come to torture us even before the judgment day, O Son of God?

30 A ways off—*though still visible, not to mention odoriferous*—was a
large herd of pigs, eating.

Demons | 31 If You cast us out *of the bodies of these two men,*
do send us into that herd of pigs!

Jesus | 32 *Very well then,* go!

And the demons flew out of the bodies *of the two flailing men,* they
set upon the pigs, and every last pig rushed over a steep bank into
the sea and drowned. 33 The pig herders *(totally undone, as you can
imagine)* took off; they headed straight for town, where they told
everyone what they'd just seen—even about the demon-possessed
men. 34 And so the whole town came out to see Jesus for themselves.
And when they saw Him, they begged Him to leave their area.

> Some people recognized that Jesus was powerful, but they wanted nothing to do with His kind of power. As in this case, it cost them dearly.

CHAPTER 9

DINNER WITH TAX COLLECTORS AND SINNERS

1 *And so Jesus decided to go home.* He got back in the boat, crossed
the sea, and returned to His own town. 2 When He got there, some
men approached Him carrying a mat. On the mat was another man,
a paralytic. *The men believed fervently that Jesus could heal the para-*
lytic, and Jesus saw their faith, how much faith they had in His
authority and power.

Jesus | Rest assured, My son; your sins are forgiven.

3 Now, some scribes *and teachers of the law had been watching this*
whole scene.

Scribes and Teachers *(to themselves)* | This man is blaspheming!

4 *Though they had only spoken in low whispers among themselves,*
Jesus knew their thoughts.

Jesus | Why do you hold such hardness and wickedness in
your hearts? 5 Look, is it easier to say, "Your sins are
forgiven," or "Get up and walk"? 6 To make clear
that the Son of Man has the authority on earth to
forgive sins (turning to the paralytic man on the
mat), Get up, pick up your mat, and go home.

[7]And the man did. [8]When the crowd saw this, they were amazed, *even a little scared,* and they praised God who had given humans the authority *to do such miraculous things.*

[9]Later, Jesus was walking along and he saw a man named Matthew sitting in the tax *collector's* office.

Jesus *(to Matthew)*	Follow Me.

Matthew got up and followed Him.

[10]*It was not, in fact, unusual for Jesus to hang out with tax collectors.* Once when He ate a meal at home with His disciples, a whole host of tax collectors and other sinners joined them. [11]When the Pharisees saw this, they asked Jesus' disciples,

Pharisees	Why does your Teacher eat with tax collectors and sinners?
Jesus *(overhearing this)*	[12]Look, who needs a doctor—healthy people or sick people? [13]I am not here to attend to people who are already right with God; I am here to attend to sinners. *In the book of the prophet Hosea, we read,* "It is not sacrifice I want, but mercy."* *Go and meditate on that for a while—maybe you'll come to understand it.*

[14]And then some of the disciples of John *the Teacher who ritually washed people* came.

John's Disciples	*What's the story with fasting?* We fast and the Pharisees fast, but Your disciples do not fast!

9:13 Hosea 6:6

Jesus | [15]When you celebrate—as at a wedding when one's dearest friend is getting married—you do not fast. The time will come when the bridegroom will be taken from them. Then My friends and followers will fast.

With these words about the bridegroom being taken from them, Jesus hinted at what lay down His narrow road. He continued with a discussion about change and patching a torn garment.

Jesus | [16]You would begin by washing and shrinking a patch you would use to mend a garment—otherwise, the patch would shrink later, pull away from the garment, and make the original tear even worse. [17]Nor would you pour new wine into old wineskins. If you did, the skins would burst, the wine would run out, and the wineskins would be ruined. No, you would pour new wine into new wineskins—and both the wine and the wineskins would be preserved.

[18]As He was saying these things, a certain official came before Jesus and knelt in front of Him.

Official | My daughter just died. Would You come and lay Your hands on her? Then, I know, she would live again.

[19]Jesus got up, and He and His disciples went with the man. [20-21]*But as they were heading to the man's house,* a woman who had been hemorrhaging and bleeding for 12 years—12 years! —crept up behind

Jesus. *She had been listening to Him teach and watching Him, so she knew that if she so much as touched the fringes of His cloak, she would be healed.* And so she came up behind Him and touched His cloak. [22]Jesus turned around and saw her.

Jesus | Take heart, daughter. Your faith has healed you.

And indeed, from that moment, the woman was healed. [23]Then Jesus went to the official's house. He saw flute players and mourners; *He saw the girl's family weeping and shocked; He saw neighbors bringing food and trying to bring comfort.*

Jesus *(to the crowd)* | [24]Go away, *and do your ministering somewhere else.* This girl is not dead. She is merely asleep.

The crowd—*who knew with certainty that the girl was dead*—laughed at Him. [25]But they *obeyed Him and* left the house, *and once they were gone,* Jesus went to the girl. *She was lying on a mat on the floor.* When He took her hand, she *opened her eyes and* stood up. [26]When the crowds outside learned that the girl was indeed alive, they spread throughout the town and the surrounding country telling everyone what had happened.

[27]Jesus left the official's house. And as He was walking, two blind men began to follow Him.

Blind Men | Son of David! Have mercy on us!

[28]Jesus went to *their* house, and the blind men sat in front of Him.

Jesus | Do you believe that I am able to do this?

Blind Men | Yes, Lord.

By now you know that it is faith in Jesus that can heal. So you will not be surprised to learn that all it took was Jesus' touch to heal these men. It was the power of Jesus that caused this miracle and not some mysterious formula or sinless life.

Jesus *(touching their eyes)* | 29 According to your faith, it will be done to you.

30 And they could see. Then Jesus spoke to them *as He had spoken to*
the leper.

Jesus | Don't tell anyone about this.

31 But when the men *(who could now see everything perfectly; every-*
thing was sharp and colorful) left, they told everyone in the area they
met what had happened.
32 Later, a man who was possessed by demons and could not talk
was brought to Jesus. 33 Jesus drove out the demons, and the mute
man spoke. The crowds were amazed.

Crowd | Nothing like this has ever been seen in Israel.

Pharisees | 34 It must be the prince of demons who gives Him the power to cast out demons.

35 Jesus went through many towns and villages. He taught in their
synagogues. He preached the good news of the kingdom of God. He
healed every disease and sickness. 36 Whenever crowds came to Him,
He had compassion for them because they were so deeply dis-
traught, malaised, and heartbroken. They seemed to Him like lost

sheep without a shepherd. 37*Jesus understood what an awesome task
was before Him*, so He said to His disciples, "The harvest is plentiful
but the workers are few. 38Ask the Lord of the harvest to send more
workers into His harvest field."

CHAPTER 10

INSTRUCTION FOR THE TWELVE

1 Jesus called His twelve disciples to Him. He endowed them with
the authority to heal sickness and disease and to drive demons out
of those who were possessed.

> Up to this point, the disciples had been, mostly, following Jesus around, listening to Him teach, watching Him heal. And so now we call these twelve beloved men not merely *disciples,* "apprentices," but *apostles,* which means "those who are sent as representatives." Jesus was preparing to send them into the harvest field to do His Father's work.

2 These are the names of the twelve apostles: Simon (who is called
Peter, *which means "the rock"*) and his brother Andrew; James, son
of Zebedee, and his brother John; 3 Philip and Bartholomew;
Thomas and Matthew (the tax collector); James, son of Alphaeus,
and Thaddaeus; 4 Simon the Zealot and Judas Iscariot (who would
betray Him).

5 Jesus sent out these twelve with clear instructions.

Jesus | Don't go to the Gentiles or to the towns inhabited
by Samaritans. 6 Go instead to find and heal the lost
sheep of Israel. 7 As you go, preach this message:
"The kingdom of heaven is at hand." 8 Heal the sick,
raise the dead, and cleanse those who have leprosy.

Drive out demons *from the possessed.* You received
these gifts freely, so you should give *them* to others
freely. [9]Do not take money with you: don't take
gold, silver, or even small, worthless change. [10]Do
not pack a bag with clothes. Do not take sandals or
a walking stick. *You must embody simplicity.* Be fed
and sheltered by those who show you hospitality,
*but never let it be said that you are working wonders
in order to get rich.*

[11]When you enter a town or village, look for
someone who is trustworthy and stay at his house
as long as you are visiting that town. [12]When you
enter this home, greet the household kindly. [13]And
if the home is indeed trustworthy, let your blessing
of peace rest upon it; if not, keep your blessing to
yourself. [14]If someone is inhospitable to you or
refuses to listen to your testimony, leave that house
or town and shake the dust from your feet. [15]This is
the truth: Sodom and Gomorrah, *those ancient pits
of inhospitality,* will fare better on judgment day
than towns *who ignore you tomorrow or next week.*

[16]Listen: I am sending you out to be sheep among
wolves. You must be as shrewd as serpents and as
innocent as doves. [17]You must be careful. You must
be discerning. You must be on your guard. There
will be men who try to hand you over to their town
councils and have you flogged in their synagogues.
[18]Because of Me, naysayers and doubters will try to
make an example out of you by trying you before
rulers and kings. *They will try to show people from
all nations that they, not I, have all authority and
power.* [19]When this happens—*when you are arrested,*

dragged to court, handed over for flogging—don't
worry about what to say or how to say it. The
words you should speak will be given to you. For at
that moment, [20]it will not be you speaking; it will
be the Spirit of your Father speaking through you.
[21]*Your task will be fraught with betrayal*: brother
will betray brother, even to the point of death;
fathers will betray their children, and children will
rebel against their fathers, even to the point of
death. [22-23]When you are persecuted in one town,
flee to the next town. This is the truth: you will not
be able to witness to every town in Israel before
the Son of Man comes. Everyone will hate you
because of Me. But remember: he who stays on the
narrow path until the end will be saved.
[24]A student is no greater than his teacher, and a
servant is never greater than his master. [25]It is suf-
ficient if the student is like his teacher and the servant like his master. If people call the head of a
house "Beelzebub," which means "devil," just
imagine what they're calling the members of his
household.
[26]Do not be afraid of those *who may taunt or persecute you*. Everything they do—even if they think
they are hiding behind closed doors—will come to
light. All their secrets will eventually be made
known. [27]And you should proclaim in the bright
light of day everything that I have whispered to
you in the dark. Whatever whispers you hear—
shout them from the rooftops of houses.
[28]Don't fear those who *aim to* kill just the body
but are unable to touch the soul. The one to fear is

he who can destroy you, soul and body, in the fires of hell. [29]Look, if you sold a few sparrows, *how much money would you get*? A copper coin apiece, perhaps? And yet your Father in heaven knows when those small sparrows fall to the ground. [30-31]You, beloved, are worth so much more than a whole flock of sparrows. God *knows everything about you*, even the number of hairs on your head. So do not fear.

[32]*Whoever knows Me here on earth, I will know him in heaven.* And whoever proclaims faith in Me here on earth, I will proclaim *faith in* him before My Father in heaven. [33]But whoever disowns Me here, I will disown before My Father in heaven.

[34]Do not imagine that I have come to bring peace to the earth. I did not come to bring peace, but a sword. [35]I have come to turn men against their fathers, daughters against their mothers, and daughters-in-law against mothers-in-law. [36]You will find you have enemies even in your own household.* [37]If you love your father or mother more than you love Me, then you are not worthy of Me. If you love your son or daughter more than you love Me, then you are not worthy of Me. [38]If you refuse to take up your cross and follow Me *on the narrow road*, then you are not worthy of Me. [39]To find your life, you must lose your life—and whoever loses his life for My sake will find it.

[40]Anyone who welcomes you welcomes Me, and anyone who welcomes Me welcomes the One who sent Me. [41]Anyone who welcomes a prophet and

10:36 Micah 7:6

surrenders to his prophecy will receive a prophet's
reward, and anyone who welcomes a righteous
person and conforms to the righteousness that sur-
rounds him and proceeds from him will receive a
righteous man's reward. 42And anyone who has so
much as given a cup of cold water to one of the little ones, because he is My disciple, I tell you, that
person will be well rewarded.

CHAPTER 11

PREPARING THE WAY FOR JESUS

1With that, Jesus finished instructing His disciples, and He went on
to preach and teach in the towns *of Galilee.*
2John the Teacher who dipped people, meanwhile, was still in
prison. But stories about the Messiah's teachings and healing
reached him.

> Quite frankly, John was perplexed. He had been awaiting the Messiah, but he believed the Messiah would be a great political ruler, a king, or a military hero. Jesus seemed to be all about healing people and insisting that the poor and the meek were blessed.

So John sent his followers 3to question Jesus.

John's Followers
Are You the One we have been expecting as Savior
for so long? *Are You the One Scripture promised
would come?* Or should we expect someone else?

Jesus
4Go back and tell John the things you have heard
and the things you have seen. 5*Tell him you have
seen* the blind receive sight, the lame walk, the lep-
ers cured, the deaf hear, the dead raised, and the
good news preached to the poor. 6Blessed are those
who *understand what is afoot and* stay on My narrow path.

[7]John's disciples left, and Jesus began to speak to a crowd about John. *He wanted to make sure people understood who they had seen when they saw John.*

Jesus | What did you go into the desert to see? Did you expect to see a reed blowing around in the wind? [8]No? Were you expecting to see a man dressed in the finest silks? No, of course not—you find silk in the sitting rooms of palaces and mansions, not in the middle of the wilderness. [9]So what did you go out to see? A prophet? Yes. Yes, a prophet and more than a prophet. [10]When you saw John, you saw the one whom the prophet *Malachi envisioned when he* said, "I will send a messenger ahead of you, and he will prepare the way for you."*

[11]This is the truth: no one has ever been born to a woman greater than John the Immersing Teacher.* And yet the most insignificant person in the kingdom of heaven is greater than he. [12-13]All of the prophets of old, all of the Law—that was all prophecy leading up to the coming of John. *Now, the time for that sort of prophecy is through. All of that prophecy and teaching was to prepare us to come to this very point, right here and now.* When John the Teacher* who ritually cleansed came, the kingdom of heaven began to break in upon us and those in power are trying to clamp down on it—*why do you think John is in jail?* [14]If only you could see it—John is the Elijah, the prophet we were

---

11:10 Malachi 3:1
11:11 Literally, John who immersed, to show repentance
11:12-13 Literally, John who immersed, to show repentance

promised would come *and prepare the way.* [15]He
who has ears *for the truth,* let him hear.

In this way, Jesus invited His followers to understand who John the Teacher was, and, in turn, who He must be.

Jesus

[16]What is this generation like? You are like children
sitting in the marketplace and calling out, [17]"When
we played the flute you did not dance, and when
we sang a dirge you did not mourn." [18]*What I mean
is this:* When John came, *he came from a place of
the wilderness. He dressed in the clothes of an outcast, and* he did not eat but lived on honey and
wild locusts. And people wondered *if he was crazy,*
if he had been possessed by a demon. [19]Then the
Son of Man appeared—He didn't fast, as John had,
but ate *with sinners* and drank *wine.* And the people said, "This Man is a glutton! He's a drunk! And
He hangs around with tax collectors and sinners,
to boot." Well, Wisdom will be vindicated by her
actions—*not by your opinions.*

[20]Then Jesus began to preach about the towns He'd visited. He'd
performed some of His most fantastic miracles *in places like
Chorazin and Bethsaida,* but still the people in those places hadn't
turned to God.

Jesus

[21]Woe to you, Chorazin! And woe to you, Bethsaida!
Had I gone to Tyre and Sidon and performed miracles there, they would have repented immediately,
taking on sackcloth and ashes. [22]But I tell you this:

the people from Tyre and Sidon will fare better on the day of judgment than you will. [23]And Capernaum! Do you think you will reign exalted in heaven? *No,* you'll rot in hell. Had I gone to Sodom and worked miracles there, *the people would have repented, and* Sodom would still be standing, *thriving, bustling.* [24]*Well, you know what happened to Sodom.* But know this—the people from Sodom will fare better on the day of judgment than you will.

[25]And then Jesus began to pray:

Jesus I praise You, Father—Lord of heaven and earth. You have revealed Your truths to the lowly *and the ignorant, the children and the crippled, the lame and the mute.* You have hidden wisdom from those who pride themselves on being so wise and learned. [26]You did this, simply, because it pleased You. [27]The Father has handed over everything to My care. No one knows the Son except the Father, and no one knows the Father except the Son—and those to whom the Son wishes to reveal the Father.

[28]Come to Me, all who are weary and burdened, and I will give you rest. [29]Put My yoke upon your shoulders—*it might appear heavy at first, but it is perfectly fitted to your curves.* Learn from Me, for I am gentle and humble of heart. *When you are yoked to Me,* your weary souls will find rest. [30]For My yoke is easy, and My burden is light.

CHAPTER 12

HEALING ON THE SABBATH

> The Sabbath is a day of rest when one creates nothing, breaks nothing, gives nothing, makes no contracts, cuts no flowers, and boils no water; it is a day set aside by the Lord to remember the creative work of God and to experience the peace of the Lord.

1The Sabbath came and Jesus walked through a field. His disciples, who were hungry, began to pick some of the grain and eat it. 2When the Pharisees saw this, they reacted.

Pharisees Look! Your disciples are breaking the law of the Sabbath!

Jesus 3Haven't you read what David did? When he and his friends were hungry, 4they went into God's house and they ate the holy bread, even though neither David nor his friends, but only priests, were allowed that bread. 5*Indeed,* have you not read that on the Sabbath priests themselves do work in the temple, breaking the Sabbath law yet remaining blameless? 6Listen, *One* who is greater than the temple is here.

7Do you not understand *what the prophet Hosea recorded,* "I desire mercy, not sacrifice."* If you

12:7 Hosea 6:6

understood *that snippet of Scripture*, you would not condemn these innocent men *for ostensibly breaking the law of the Sabbath.* [8]For the Son of Man *has not only the authority to heal and cast out demons,* He also has authority over the Sabbath.

[9]Jesus left the field and He went to the synagogue, [10]and there He met a man with a shriveled hand. The Pharisees wanted to set up Jesus.

Pharisees Well, is it lawful to heal on the Sabbath, too?

Jesus [11]Look, imagine that one of you has a sheep that falls into a ditch on the Sabbath—*what would you do?*

Jesus—who could see that the Pharisees were testing Him and basically missed the point—was growing a little testy. The Pharisees said nothing. Each was secretly thinking that he, of course, would dive in and get his sheep.

Jesus *(to the Pharisees)* You would dive in and rescue your sheep. [12]Now, what is more valuable, a person or a sheep? *So what do you think—should I heal this man on the Sabbath?* Isn't it lawful to do good deeds on the Sabbath?

Jesus *(to the man with the shriveled hand)* [13]Stretch out your hand.

As the man did so, his hand was completely healed, as good as new.

14The Pharisees went and mapped out plots to destroy Jesus.
15Jesus knew *that the Pharisees were plotting to kill Him—so He*
followed His own advice (the advice He had given the apostles) and
left the area. Many people followed Him, and He healed them all,
16always insisting that they tell no one about Him. 17He did this in
keeping with the prophecy Isaiah made so long ago:

18"This is My servant, whom I have *well* chosen;
  this is the One I love, the One in whom I delight.
I will place My Spirit upon Him;
  He will proclaim justice to all the world.
19He will not fight or shout
  or talk loudly in the streets.
20He will not crush a reed under His heel
  or blow out a smoldering candle
until He has led justice *and righteousness* to final victory.
21 All the world will find its hope in His name."*

22Some of the faithful brought Jesus a man who was possessed by
a demon, who was blind and mute, and Jesus healed him. The man
could see and talk, *and demons no longer crawled around in him.*

People *(astonished)*	23Could this be the Son of David?
Pharisees	24It is only through Beelzebul, the prince of demons, that this Jesus can cast out demons.

> What they were thinking simply made no sense. Satan glories in every demoniac, every possessed mute, every incubus who corrupts a righteous person. Why would Satan wish to drive demons out of the possessed?

12:21 Isaiah 42:1-4

25Jesus knew what the Pharisees were thinking.

Jesus That would be like a father splitting his own household down the middle or a king cutting his kingdom
in half—the household and the kingdom would fall
apart. 26So, too, if Satan *imbued people with the power*
to drive out demons, Satan's kingdom would collapse. 27And you should think about this, too: you
have friends who drive out demons. If I am working
as a tool of Beelzebul, who are your people working
for? 28When I come to you and drive out demons by
the Spirit of your Father in heaven—*for the glory of*
your Father in heaven—you should recognize and
rejoice that the kingdom of God has come to you.

29Imagine you wanted to break into the house of
your neighbor, a strong brawny man, and steal his
furniture. First, you'd have to tie up your neighbor,
yes? Once he was bound and tied, you could take
whatever you wanted. 30*Similarly*—he who is not
with Me is against Me, and he who is not *doing the*
Father's work of gathering *up the flock* may as well
be scattering *the flock.*

31-32It is one thing for you to speak ill of the Son
of Man. People will be forgiven for every sin they
commit and blasphemy they utter. *But those who*
call the work of God the work of Satan utterly
remove themselves from God, and those who blas-
pheme God's Spirit will not be forgiven, neither in
this world nor in the world to come.

33Good trees produce good fruits; bad trees produce bad fruits. You can always tell a tree by its
fruits.

[34]You children of snakes, you who are evil—how could you possibly say anything good? For the mouth simply shapes the heart's impulses into words. [35]And so the good man (who is filled with goodness) speaks good words, while the evil man (who is filled with evil) speaks evil words. [36]I tell you this: on the day of judgment, people will be called to account for every careless word they have ever said. [37]*The righteous* will be acquitted by their own words, and *you evildoers* will be condemned by your own words.

Teachers of the Law and Pharisees [38]Teacher, we want to see some miraculous sign from You.

Jesus [39]You wicked and promiscuous generation—you are looking for signs, *are you*? The only sign you will be given is the sign of the prophet Jonah. [40]Jonah spent three days and three nights in the belly of a great fish, as the Son of Man will spend three days and three nights in the belly of the earth. [41]One day, the people of Nineveh will rise up in judgment and will condemn your present generation—for the Ninevites turned from sin to God when they heard Jonah preach, and now One far greater than Jonah is here. [42]The Queen of the South will also stand in judgment and condemn this generation—for she came from the ends of the earth to listen to Solomon's wisdom. And today, One greater and wiser than Solomon is among you.

[43]*Let Me tell you what will happen to this wicked generation:* When an evil spirit comes out of a man,

it rattles around through *deserts and other* dry places looking for a place to rest—but it does not find anywhere to rest. [44]So the spirit says, "I will return to the house I left." And it returns to find that house unoccupied, tidy, swept, and sparkling clean. [45]*Well, then* not only does one spirit set up shop in that sparkling house, but it brings seven even more wicked spirits along. And the poor man—the house—is worse off than he was before. Similarly, this evil generation *will be inhabited.*

[46]While Jesus was speaking to the crowd, His mother and brothers came up and wanted to speak to Him.

Someone in the Crowd [47]Your mother and brothers are waiting outside to speak to You.

Jesus [48]Who is My mother? And who are My brothers?

Jesus *(pointing to His disciples)* [49]These are My mother and brothers. [50]Anyone who does the will of My Father in heaven is My mother and brother and sister.

CHAPTER 13

SPEAKING IN PARABLES

You're probably sensing that by now, large crowds flocked to Jesus wherever He went. This was quickly becoming the case. Sometimes these large groups made it difficult for Him to teach.

1 That same day, Jesus left the house and went to sit by the sea.
2 Large crowds gathered around Him, and He got into a boat on the
sea and sat there. The crowd stood on the shore *waiting for His
teaching.*
3 And so Jesus began to teach. *On this day,* He spoke in parables.
Here is His first parable:

Jesus | Once there was a sower who scattered seeds. 4 One
day he walked in a field scattering seeds as he
went. Some seeds fell beside a road, and a flock of
birds came and ate all those seeds. 5 *So the sower
scattered seeds in a field,* one with shallow soil and
strewn with rocks. But the seeds grew quickly
amid all the rocks, 6 without rooting themselves in
the shallow soil. Their roots got tangled up in all
the stones. The sun scorched these seeds, and they
died. 7 *And so the sower scattered seeds near a path,*
this one covered with thorny vines. *The seeds fared
no better there*—the thorns choked them, *and they
died.* 8 *And so finally the sower scattered his seeds in*

a patch of good earth. *At home in the good earth, the seeds grew and grew. Eventually,* the seeds bore fruit, *and the fruit grew ripe and was harvested. The harvest was immense*—30, 60, 100 times *what was sown.*

9 He who has ears to hear, let him hear.

Disciples 10 Why do You speak to the people in parables?

Jesus 11 The knowledge of the secrets of heaven has been given to you, but it has not been given to them. 12 Those who have something will be given more—and they will have abundance. Those who have nothing will lose what they have—*they will be destitute.* 13 I teach in parables so the people may look but not see, listen but not hear or understand.* 14 They are fulfilling Isaiah's prophecy:

> "You will listen, but you will not understand;
> You will look, but you will not see.
> 15 The people's hearts have turned to flab;
> Their ears are clogged;
> Their eyes are shut.
> They will try to see, but they will not see;
> They will try to hear, but they will not hear;
> They will try to understand, but they will not comprehend.
> *If they, with their blindness and deafness, so choose,* then I will heal them."*

16-17 Many holy prophets and righteous men and women *and people of prayer and doers of good* have

13:13 Psalm 78:2
13:15 Isaiah 6:9-10

wanted to see but did not see, and have wanted to
hear but did not hear. Your eyes and ears are blessed.
[18]This is what the parable of the sower means.
[19]*It is about the kingdom of heaven.* When someone
hears the story of the Kingdom and cannot understand it, the evil one comes and snatches away whatever *goodness and holiness* had been sown in the heart. This is like the seeds sown beside the
road. [20-21]You know people who hear the word of
God and receive it joyfully—but then, somehow, the word fails to take root in their hearts. It is temporary. As soon as God's word causes trouble for those people, they trip: *your friend who left her husband as soon as things got rocky; your friend who listened rapturously to a teaching about trusting God, but refused to take a risk when a risk was called for*—those people are the seeds strewn on
the rocky soil. [22]And you know people who hear
the word, but it is choked inside them because they constantly worry and prefer the wealth and pleasures of the world: *they prefer drunken dinner parties to prayer, power to piety, and riches to righteousness.* Those people are like the seeds sown
among thorns. [23]The people who hear the word
and receive it and grow in it—those are like the seeds sown on good soil. They produce a bumper crop, 30 or 60 or 100 times what was sown. *Your Father in heaven must plant many seeds in order to ensure that some seeds bear fruit. The final harvest, however, is worth whatever the toil.*

[24]Jesus told them another parable.

Jesus The kingdom of heaven is like this: Once there was
a farmer who sowed good seeds in his field.
25 While the farmer's workers were sleeping, his
enemy crept into the field and sowed weeds among
all the wheat seeds. Then he snuck away again.
26 Eventually the crops grew—wheat, but also
weeds. 27 So the farmer's workers said to him, "Sir,
why didn't you sow good seeds in your field?
Where did these weeds come from?"
28 "My enemy must have done this," replied the
farmer.

"Should we go pull up all the weeds?" asked his workers.

29 "No," said the farmer. "*It's too risky*. As you pull
up the weeds, you would probably pull up some
wheat as well. 30 We'll let them both grow until harvesttime. I will tell the harvesters to collect the
weeds and tie them in bundles to be burned, and
only then to harvest the wheat and bring it to my
barn."

31 Jesus told them another parable.

Jesus The kingdom of heaven is like a mustard seed,
which a sower took and planted in his field.
32 Mustard seeds are minute, tiny—but the seeds
grow into trees. Flocks of birds can come and build
their nests in the branches.

33 And Jesus told a *fourth* parable about *a baker adding leaven to change what would be flat and uninteresting into a valuable commodity. (Normally leaven has a negative connotation.)*

Jesus | *Imagine a woman preparing a loaf of bread.* The kingdom of heaven is like the leaven she folds into her dough. She kneads and kneads until the leaven is worked into all the dough. *Without the leaven, the dough remains flat. But the secret is the almost invisible leaven making her loaves fluff and rise.*

[34]Jesus gave all these teachings to the crowd in parables. Indeed,
He spoke only in parables [35]in fulfillment of the prophetic words *of the Psalms:*

"I will open My mouth in parables;
I will tell them things that have been hidden and obscure
since the very beginning of the world."*

[36]Then Jesus left the crowds and returned to His house. His disciples followed Him.

Disciples | Explain to us the story You told about the weeds.

Jesus | [37]The one who sowed the good seed is the Son of
Man. [38]The field is the world; the good seed represents the children of the Kingdom. The weeds—*who do you think the weeds are?* They are the children of the evil one, [39]and the enemy who threw the weeds among the wheat is the devil. The harvest is the end of the age, and the workers are
God's angels. [40]*In the parable,* I told you the weeds would be pulled up and burned—well, that is how
it will be at the end of this age. [41]The Son of Man will send His angels out into the world, and they will root out from His kingdom everything that is

---

13:35 Psalm 78:2

poisonous, ugly, and malicious, and everyone who
does evil. [42]They will throw all that wickedness
into the fiery furnace where there will be weeping
and grinding of teeth. [43]And the righteous will
shine like the sun in their Father's kingdom. He
who has ears to hear, let him hear.

[44]The kingdom of heaven is like a treasure that is
hidden in a field. A *crafty* man found the treasure
buried there and buried it again *so no one would
know where it was*. Thrilled, he went off and sold
everything he had, and then he came back and
bought the field *with the hidden treasure part of the
bargain*.

[45]Or, the kingdom of heaven is like a jeweler on
the lookout for the finest pearls. [46]When he found a
pearl more beautiful and valuable than any jewel
he had ever seen, the jeweler sold all he had and
bought that pearl, *his pearl of great price*.

[47]Or *think of it this way*: the kingdom of heaven
is like a net that was cast into the sea, a net that
caught a world of flickering fish. [48]When the net
was full, the fishermen hauled it to shore. They
separated the good fish from the bad, placing the
good fish in a bucket and throwing out the inedible
fish. [49]That is what the end of time will be like. The
angels will separate *the good from the bad*, the
righteous from the wicked, *the repentant from the
prideful, the faithful from the hard-hearted*. [50]*The
bad, the wicked, the prideful, and the hard-hearted*
will be thrown into the fiery furnace where there
will be weeping and grinding of teeth.

[51]Do you understand?

Disciples | Yes, *we understand.*

Jesus | [52]Every scribe *and teacher of the law* who has become a student of the ways of the Kingdom is like the head of the household who brings some new things and some old things, both out of the storeroom.

[53]With that Jesus finished teaching His parables, and He moved
on. [54-56]He came to *Nazareth*, the town where He had grown up. He
taught at the local synagogue, and the people were astonished.

People | *Is this our little Jesus?* Is this Mary's son? Is this the carpenter's son? Is this Jesus, brother of James, Joseph, Simon, and Judas? Didn't we just see His sisters *yesterday at the market*? Where did He learn all this? Whence His power?

[57]They were offended by Him—*by His teachings, by His presumptuousness, by His bearing, by His very self.*

Jesus | Prophets are respected—except in their hometowns and in their own households. *There, the prophet is dishonored.*

[58]Jesus didn't bother to work wondrous miracles there *in Nazareth* because the people did not believe.

CHAPTER 14

HEROD AND JOHN; JESUS FEEDS 5,000

1At this time, the ruler *of Galilee* was Herod *Antipas*. He began to
hear reports about all that Jesus was doing.
2*Like the people of Nazareth,* Herod wondered where Jesus' power
came from.

Herod *(to his servants)* | He must be John the Teacher who washed ceremonially,* raised from the dead; thus His power.

> Herod was quite concerned with the attention that John the Teacher was receiving, but he didn't want to spend precious political capital killing a reputed holy man. On top of that, Jesus was beginning to create an even greater problem for Herod.

3-5Herod's brother Philip had married a woman named Herodias,
who eventually married Herod. John denounced Herod's marriage to
her as adulterous. Herod was incensed *(not to mention a little fear-
ful)* and wanted to kill John, but he knew the people considered
John a prophet. Instead, he bound John and put him in jail.
6-7*There John sat until* Herod's birthday. On that night, *Salome,*
Herodias's daughter *by Philip,* came and danced for her stepfather
and all his birthday guests. Herod so enjoyed her dancing that he
vowed to give her whatever she wanted.

14:2 Literally, John who immersed, to show repentance

Salome *(after whispering with her mother)*

8Bring me the head of John the Teacher and
Prophet,* displayed on a platter.

> *T*his was not what Herod had expected—he'd imagined his step-daughter might ask for a necklace or maybe a slave.

9Herod still thought it unwise to kill John, but *because he had*
made such a show of his promise—because he had actually sworn an
oath and *because the scene was playing out* in front of *the watchful*
eyes of so many guests—Herod felt bound *to give his stepdaughter*
what she wanted. 10And so he sent orders to the prison to have John
beheaded, 11and there was his head, displayed on a platter, given first
to *Salome* and then passed on to her mother.

12John's disciples went to the prison, got John's body, and buried
him. Then they went to tell Jesus.

13When Jesus learned what had happened, He got on a boat and
went away to spend some time in a private place. The crowds, of
course, followed Jesus, on foot from their cities. 14*Though Jesus*
wanted solitude, when He saw the crowds, He had compassion on
them, and He healed the sick *and the lame.* 15At evening-time, Jesus'
disciples came to Him.

Disciples

We're in a fairly remote place, and it is getting late; *the crowds will get hungry for supper*. Send them away so they have time to get back to the village and get something to eat.

Jesus

16They don't need to go back to the village in order
to eat supper. Give them something to eat here.

14:8 Literally, John who immersed, to show repentance

Disciples [17]*But we don't have enough food.* We only have five rounds *of flatbread* and two fish.

Jesus [18]Bring the bread and the fish to Me.

So the disciples brought Him the five rounds of flatbread, and the two fish, [19]and Jesus told the people to sit down on the grass. He took the bread and the fish, He looked up to heaven, He gave thanks, and then He broke the bread. Jesus gave the bread to the disciples, and the disciples gave the bread to the people; [20]everyone ate and was satisfied. *When everyone had eaten,* the disciples picked up 12 baskets *of crusts and broken pieces of bread and crumbs. Not only was there enough, but there was an abundance.* [21]There were 5,000 men there, not to mention all the women and children.

[22]Immediately, Jesus made the disciples get into the boat and go on to the other side of the sea while He dismissed the crowd. [23]Then, after the crowd had gone, Jesus went up to a mountaintop alone (*as He had intended from the start*). As evening descended, He stood alone on the mountain, praying. [24]The boat was in the water, some distance from land, buffeted and pushed around by waves and wind.

[25]Deep in the night, *when He had concluded His prayers,* Jesus walked out on the water to His disciples *in their boat.* [26]The disciples saw a figure moving toward them and were terrified.

Disciple It's a ghost!

Another Disciple A ghost? What will we do?

Jesus [27] Be still. It is I. You have nothing to fear.

Peter [28]Lord, if it is really You, then command me to meet You on the water.

Jesus | [29]*Indeed,* come.

Peter stepped out of the boat onto the water and began walking toward Jesus. [30]But when he remembered how strong the wind was, his courage caught in his throat and he began to sink.

Peter | Master, save me!

[31]Immediately, Jesus reached for Peter and caught him.

Jesus | O you of little faith. Why did you doubt *and dance back and forth between following* Me *and heeding fear*?

[32]Then Jesus and Peter climbed in the boat together, and the wind became still. [33]And the disciples worshiped Him.

Disciples | Truly You are the Son of God.

[34]All together, Jesus and the disciples crossed *to the other side of the sea.* They landed at Gennesaret, *an area famous for its princely gardens.* [35]The people of Gennesaret recognized Jesus, and they spread word of His arrival all over the countryside. People brought the sick *and wounded* to Him [36]and begged Him for permission to touch the fringes of His robe. Everyone who touched Him was healed.

Matthew

Chapter 15

WHAT MAKES YOU CLEAN?

1 Some Pharisees and scribes came from Jerusalem to ask Jesus a
question.

Scribes and Pharisees | 2 The law of Moses has always held that one must
ritually wash his hands before eating. Why don't
Your disciples observe this tradition?

3 Jesus—*who was developing a reputation as One who gave as good
as He got*—turned the Pharisees' question back on them.

Jesus | Why do you violate God's command because of your
tradition? 4 God said, "Honor your father and mother.* Anyone who curses his father or mother must
be put to death."* 5-6 But you say that one need no
longer honor his parents so long as he says to them,
"What you might have gained from me, I now give
to the glory of God." Haven't you let your tradition
trump the word of God? 7 You hypocrites! Isaiah
must have had you in mind when he prophesied,

8 "People honor Me with their lips,
But their hearts are nowhere near Me.
9 Because they elevate mere human ritual to the
status of law,
Their worship of Me is a meaningless sham."*

15:4 Exodus 20:12; Deuteronomy 5:16
15:4 Leviticus 20:9
15:9 Isaiah 29:13

10(To the multitude) Hear and understand this:
11What you put into your mouth cannot make you
clean or unclean—it is what comes out of your
mouth that can make you unclean.

12Later, the disciples came to Him.

Disciples Do You realize the Pharisees were shocked by
what You said?

Jesus 13Every plant planted by someone other than My
heavenly Father will be plucked up by the roots.
14So let them be. They are blind guides. What happens when one blind person leads another? Both of
them fall into a ditch.

Peter 15Explain that riddle to us.

Jesus 16Do you still not see? 17Don't you understand that
whatever you take in through your mouth makes
its way to your stomach and eventually out *of the
bowels* of your body? 18But the things that come out
of your mouth—*your curses, your fears, your denun-
ciations*—these come from your heart, and it is the
stirrings of your heart that can make you unclean.
19For your heart harbors evil thoughts—fantasies of
murder, adultery, and whoring; fantasies of steal-
ing, lying, and slandering. 20These make you
unclean—not eating with a hand you've not ritually
purified with a splash of water *and a prayer*.

21Jesus left that place and withdrew to Tyre and Sidon. 22A Canaanite woman—*a non-Jew*—came to Him.

Canaanite Woman *(wailing)* | Lord, Son of David, have mercy on me! My daughter is possessed by a demon. *Her body is wracked! Her mind is senseless! Have mercy, Lord!*

23Jesus said nothing. *And the woman continued to wail.* His disciples came to Him.

Disciples | Do something—she keeps crying after us!

Jesus | 24I was sent here only to gather up the lost sheep of Israel.

25The woman came up to Jesus and knelt before Him.

Canaanite Woman | Lord, help me!

Jesus | 26It is not right to waste your children's bread feeding dogs.

Canaanite Woman | 27But, Lord, even dogs eat the crumbs that fall by the table as their master is eating.

28Jesus—whose ancestors included Ruth and Rahab—spoke with kindness and insight.

Jesus | Woman, you have great faith. And your request is done.

And her daughter was healed, right then and from then on.

29Jesus left and went to the Sea of Galilee. He went up on a mountaintop and sat down. 30Crowds thronged to Him there, bringing the lame, *the maimed,* the blind, the crippled, the mute, and many other

sick and broken people. They laid them at His feet, and He healed
them. [31]The people saw the mute speaking, the lame walking, *the*
maimed made whole, the crippled dancing, and the blind seeing; and
the people were amazed, and they praised the God of Israel.

Jesus *(to His disciples)*
[32]*We must take pity on* these people for they have
touched My heart—they have been with Me for
three days, and they don't have any food. I don't
want to send them home this hungry—they might
collapse on the way!

Disciples
[33]We'll never find enough food for all these people,
out here in the middle of nowhere!

Jesus
[34]How much bread do you have?

Disciples
Seven *rounds of flatbread* and a few small fish.

[35]He told the crowd to sit down. [36]He took the bread and the fish,
He gave thanks, and then He broke the bread and divided the fish.
He gave the bread and fish to the disciples, the disciples distributed
them to the people, [37]and everyone ate and was satisfied. When
everyone had eaten, the disciples picked up seven baskets *of crusts*
and *broken pieces and crumbs. Not only was there enough, but there*
was an abundance. [38]There were 4,000 men there, not to mention all
the women and children.

[39]Then Jesus sent the crowd away. He got into His boat and went
to Magadan.

CHAPTER 16

WHO DO YOU SAY I AM?

Now at this time in Judea, the Jews, the children of Israel, were a diverse bunch. One group of Jews, which you have already read about, was called the Pharisees. Another family of Jews was called the Sadducees. The two groups did not agree about how to read Scripture; they did not see eye-to-eye, and they did not get along. They rarely partnered with each other. But here we find them partnering—because they were so perplexed, befuddled, and panicked about this Jesus.

1They came to Him together, a band of Pharisees and a band of Sadducees, trying to trick and trap Him. They asked Him for a sign from heaven.

Jesus 2At evening time, you read the sky as a sign—you
say, "The weather will be fine because the sky is
shading red," 3and in the morning, *you read the sky*
as a sign saying, "The red, stormy sky tells me that
today we will have storms." So you are skilled at
interpreting the sky, but you cannot interpret the
signs of the times? 4Only a cheating and evil generation *such as this* would beg for a miraculous sign
from heaven. The only sign you will get will be the
sign of Jonah.

Here again, Jesus hinted at what was to happen to Him. He spoke into the situation at hand while revealing the plan of God.

And then Jesus left them and went away.

[5]When next the disciples crossed *the Sea of Galilee,* they forgot to bring any bread with them.

Jesus | [6]Be careful, avoid the leaven of the Pharisees and Sadducees.

[7]The disciples *were not quite sure what Jesus meant,* so they discussed His warning among themselves.

Disciples | *He must mean not to buy any bread from a baker who associates with the Pharisees or Sadducees.* He must have given us this warning because we showed up here without any bread.

[8]Jesus knew what the disciples were saying among themselves, *and He took them to task.*

Jesus | You men of little faith, *do you really think that I care which baker you patronize? After spending so much time with Me, do you still not understand what I mean?* So you showed up without bread, why talk about it?—[9-10]Don't you remember that we fed 5,000 men with five rounds of flatbread? Don't you remember that we fed 4,000 men with seven rounds of bread? Don't you remember what excess, what abundance there was—*how many broken pieces and crusts you collected after everyone had eaten and was* *sated*? [11]So when I speak about leaven, I am not talking about what we will eat for dinner. I say again, avoid the leaven of the Pharisees and Sadducees.

[12]And then the disciples understood: Jesus was not talking about the bread you eat, *but about the food that feeds your soul. He was speaking in metaphor;* He was warning them against imbibing the teachings of the Pharisees and Sadducees.

[13]Jesus then went to Caesarea Philippi.

Jesus *(to His disciples)* Who do people say the Son of Man is?

Disciples [14]Some say John who ritually cleanses people.* And some say Elijah. And some say Jeremiah or one of the other prophets.

Jesus [15]And you? Who do you say that I am?

Simon Peter [16]You are the Christ. You are the Son of the living God.

Jesus [17]Simon, son of Jonah, your knowledge is a mark of blessing. For you didn't learn this truth from your friends or from teachers or from sages you've met on the way. You learned it from My Father in heaven. [18]This is why I have called you Peter *(rock)* for on this rock I will build My church. The church will reign triumphant even at the gates of hell. [19]Peter, I give you the keys to the kingdom of heaven. Whatever you bind on earth will be bound in heaven, and whatever you loose on earth will be loosed in heaven.

16:14 Literally, John who immersed, to show repentance

Christ is the foundation, and Peter with his confession of Jesus as the Christ is how the church will be built. The promise to Peter is for the church as it is opposed by various forces. He says that nothing will overcome the church, not the powers of doubt and deception that come from within, and not even death can stop it. Jesus' words to Peter are the beginning of the church. The beginning of the Kingdom is here, now.

20 And Jesus ordered His disciples *to keep these teachings secret.*

Jesus | You must tell no one that I am the Messiah.

21 Then Jesus began to tell the disciples *about what would happen
to Him. He said* He would have to go to Jerusalem, and there the
elders, chief priests, and scribes would meet Him, He would suffer
at their hands, and He would be killed. But three days later, He
would be raised *to new life.*
22 *As Jesus spoke of the things to come,* Peter took Him aside. *Sad
and confused, and maybe a little bit prideful,* Peter chastised Jesus.

Peter | No, Lord! Never! These things that You are saying—they will never happen to You!

Jesus *(turning to Peter)* | 23 Get away from Me, Satan!

This, you will recall, was the very thing He said to the devil during those wilderness temptations.

Jesus: You are a stumbling block before Me! You are not thinking about God's story—you are thinking about *some distorted story of fallen, broken* people.

Jesus *(to all His disciples)*: If you want to follow Me, you must deny yourself *the things you think you want*. You must pick up your cross and follow Me. 25The person who wants to save his life must lose it, and she who loses her life for Me will find it. 26Look, does it make sense to truly become successful, but then to hand over your very soul? What is your soul really worth? 27The Son of Man will come in His Father's glory, with His angels, and then He will reward each person for what has been done. 28I tell you this: some of you standing here, you will see the Son of Man come into His kingdom before you taste death.

> Jesus is providing an entirely different perspective on success and happiness. The new Kingdom is breaking in, and the new community is coming together. This is the logic of that Kingdom and that community: if you want to inhabit God's story, this is what you must do. To accrue fame and comfort and riches and love is counter to this new community. In the mathematics and logic of this new community, real success is measured spiritually and the promised rewards are immense.

CHAPTER 17

JESUS, MOSES, AND ELIJAH

1Six days later, Jesus went up to the top of a high mountain with
Peter, James, and John. 2There, *something spectacular happened:*
Jesus' face began to glow and gleam and shine like the morning sun.
His clothes gleamed, too—bright white, like sunlight *mirroring off a*
snowfall. He was, *in a word,* transfigured. 3Suddenly there at the top
of the mountain were Moses and Elijah, *those icons of the faith,*
beloved of God. And they talked to Jesus. *The three men stood at the intersection of heaven and earth; they were gleaming, talking.*

Peter | 4Lord, how amazing that we are here *to see these heroes of our faith, these men through whom God spoke.* Should I quickly build some shelter, three *small* tabernacles, for You, for Moses, and for Elijah?

5As Peter spoke, a bright cloud enveloped all of them.

Voice from the Cloud | This is My beloved Son. With Him I am well pleased. Listen to Him.

> You will remember: this was but an echo of the Voice that spoke at Jesus' ceremonial washing. It is an echo of what God said through Moses during his final sermon on the mount. God promised that although Moses could not enter the promised land, He would send His

people another prophet. Moses' very last wish for his beloved people was that they would listen to this new prophet when He came.

[6]This voice from heaven terrified the three disciples, and they fell prostrate on the ground. [7]But Jesus—*who was, by this time, used to His disciples' being plagued by fear*—touched them.

Jesus | Get up. Don't be afraid.

[8]And when the disciples got up, they saw they were alone with their Lord. *Moses and Elijah had returned from where they came.*

[9]The four men hiked back down the mountain, and Jesus told His disciples to stay silent.

Jesus | Don't tell anyone what happened here, not until the Son of Man has been raised from the dead.

Why was Jesus always telling His disciples to keep secrets? Perhaps because He knew that they would not understand the meaning of the transfiguration until they had lived through that other hilltop event, the death of Jesus on the cross. We, like the disciples, will better understand this bath of light and revelation when we come to Golgotha and the cross.

Disciples | [10]Master, why do the scribes teach that the prophet Elijah must come before the Messiah?

Jesus | [11]*The teachers of the Law are not wrong: our sacred Scripture tells us clearly that indeed* Elijah will come to restore all things. [12]But see this: Elijah has come already. No one recognized him for who he was, so he was arrested and killed. *That is part of the preparation of which our Scripture speaks*: for the Son of Man, too, will be arrested and killed at the hands of people *who do not see Him for who He is.*

[13]And then the disciples realized the man they knew as John the
Teacher from the wilderness* was the one Jesus was speaking of *as the fulfillment of the prophet Elijah's role—he who prepared the way for the coming of the Lord.*

[14]*They had come down from the mountain, and as they headed
toward town,* they came to a crowd. As they approached the crowd, a man rushed up to Jesus and knelt before Him.

Man from the Crowd

[15]Lord, have mercy on my son. He has seizures.
They are uncontrollable, unpredictable, wholly unmanageable, and sometimes when they come on, my son falls into the fire or into a pond. *We are sure he will one day be burned to a crisp or will drown in the sea or will shake to death.* [16]I brought
him to Your disciples, but they could not heal him.

Jesus was furious—not at the man, perhaps, but with His disciples who could have healed the boy if only they'd had enough faith.

Jesus

[17]This generation is *no better than the generation who wandered in the desert,* who lost faith and bowed down *to golden idols as soon as Moses disappeared upon Mt. Sinai!* How long will I have to shepherd these unbelieving sheep? *(Turning to the man)* Bring the boy to Me.

17:13 Literally, John who immersed, to show repentance

[18]*The man did, and* Jesus castigated the demon who had taken up residence in the boy. And the demon fled the boy's body *at the sound of Jesus' voice,* and the boy was healed from that moment on. *No more shaking. No more falling into fires.*

[19]*Later,* when they were away from the crowds, the disciples asked Jesus why they hadn't been able to drive out the demon themselves.

Jesus | [20]Because you have so little faith. I tell you this: *if you had even a faint spark of faith,* even faith *as tiny as* a mustard seed, you could say to this mountain, "Move from here to there," and, *because of your faith,* the mountain would move. *If you had just a sliver of faith,* you would find nothing impossible. [[21]But this kind is not realized except through much prayer and fasting.]*

[22]Jesus and the disciples came to Galilee.

Jesus | The Son of Man is going to be betrayed into the hands of men. [23]They will kill Him, and on the third day, He will be resurrected, *vindicated, newly alive.*

The disciples were filled with grief.

[24]Then Jesus and His disciples went toward Capernaum, and when they arrived there, some people who had collected the two-drachma tax *that went for the upkeep of the temple* came up to Peter.

Temple Tax Collectors | Does your Teacher not pay the *temple* tax?

17:21 Verse 21 is omitted in the earliest manuscripts.

Peter | [25]He does pay the tax.

Jesus knew that He and His followers were the true temple, and yet Jesus was canny. It was not quite time to shake the foundations of the temple or of the old way of doing things. And so He would pay the tax and bide His time.

So when Peter came into the house where they were staying, Jesus explored the subject.

Jesus | Simon, what do you think? When kings collect taxes and duties and tolls, from whom do they collect—do they levy taxes on their own people or on strangers and foreigners?

Peter | [26]The foreigners, my Lord.

Jesus | Well, then, we children of the King should be exempt from this two-drachma tax. [27]But all in all, it's better not to make any waves; *we'd better go on and pay the tax*. So do this: go out to the lake and throw out your line. And when you catch a fish, open its jaws and you will find a four-drachma coin. Take this to the tax collectors and pay your taxes, and Mine.

CHAPTER 18

LOST SHEEP AND FORGIVENESS

The disciples struggled with the concept of the kingdom of heaven. They did not yet understand that in the arithmetic of the new Kingdom to even consider who was most important or most powerful was a contradiction in terms.

1Around that same time, the disciples came to Jesus and questioned Him about the kingdom of heaven.

A Disciple | In the kingdom of heaven, who is the greatest?

2Jesus called over a little child. *He put His hand on the top of the child's head.*

Jesus | 3This is the truth: unless you change and become
like little children, you will never enter the kingdom of heaven. 4In that kingdom, the most humble
who are most like this child are the greatest.
5And whoever welcomes a child, *whoever wel-*
comes the weak and the friendless, the small and the
frail, the mute and the poor, the ugly and disfigured—
whoever welcomes those in My name, welcomes Me.
6And do not lead astray one of the weak and friendless who believes in Me. *Do not plant doubt, or*
tempt, or in any way lure her from Me. If you do, it

would be better for you to be dragged down with a
millstone and drowned in the bottom of the sea.

7Beware indeed of those in a world filled with
obstacles and temptations *that cause people to turn
away from Me.* Those temptations are woven into
the fabric of a world *not yet redeemed*; but beware
to anyone who lures righteous women and men off
the narrow path. 8If your hand constantly grasps at
the things of this world rather than serves the
Kingdom—cut it off and throw it away. If your foot
is always leading you to wander, then cut it off and
throw it away; it is better for you to hobble, crippled, into the *kingdom of* life than to burn in hell
with two hands and two feet. 9And if your eye
always focuses on things that cause you to sin, then
pull your eye out and throw it away. It is better for
you to see *the kingdom of* life with one eye than to
see the fires of hell *with perfect sight.*

10Make sure that you do not look down on the
little ones, *on those who struggle, on those who are
further behind you on the path of righteousness.* For
I tell you: they are watched over by those *most
beloved* angels who are always in the company of
My Father in heaven. 11[The Son of Man has come
to save all those who are lost.]* 12A shepherd in
charge of 100 sheep notices that one of his sheep
has gone astray. What do you think he should do?
Should the shepherd leave the flock on the hills
unguarded to search for the lost sheep? *God's shepherd goes to look for that one lost sheep,* 13*and* when
he finds her, he is happier about her return than he

18:11 Verse 11 is omitted in the earliest manuscripts.

is about the 99 who stayed put. [14]Your Father in heaven does not want a single one of the *tripped, waylaid, stumbling* little ones to be lost.

This wisdom of the world would tell that the shepherd should forget that one missing sheep and chalk it up as a loss because the sheep was not worth the time he'd spend chasing her down. The arithmetic of heaven's value works differently. In God's economy, each soul has its own value apart from all others.

Jesus [15]This is what you do if one of your brothers or sisters sins against you: go to him, in private, and tell him just what you perceive the wrong to be. If he listens to you, you've won a brother. [16]*But sometimes he will not listen.* And if he does not listen, go back, taking a friend or two friends with you *(for, as we have learned in Deuteronomy*, every matter of communal import should be testified to by two or three witnesses).* [17]Then, if your brother or sister still refuses to heed, you are to share what you know with the entire church, and if your brother or sister still refuses to listen to the entire church, you are to cast out your unrepentant sibling and consider them no different from Gentiles and tax collectors.

It is essential to remember the entire teaching of this passage. Reflect on the beginning of this passage, on the lost sheep; remember that what God desires most is not the rebuke of sin for the sake of the

18:16 Deuteronomy 19:15

rebuke, but loving chastisement for the sake of bringing the sinful back to God. Casting out an unrepentant member is only a last resort.

Jesus [18]Remember this: whatever you bind on earth will
be bound in heaven, and whatever you loose on
earth will be loosed in heaven. [19]And this: if two *or*
three of you come together as a community *and*
discern clearly about anything, My Father in heav-
en will bless that discernment. [20]For when two or
three gather together in My name, I am there in
the midst of them.

Peter [21]Lord, when someone has sinned against me, how
many times ought I forgive him? *Once? Twice?* As
many as seven times?

Jesus [22]You must forgive not seven times, but seventy
times seven.

The response of Jesus is like the story of Lamech in Genesis. Lamech was Adam and Eve's great-great-great-great-grandson. He had two wives. And one day he said to his wives, "Wives, listen to me: once a young man wounded me, and I killed him. You see, I will be avenged seventy-seven times."* In this new Kingdom of forgiveness, we reverse and inverse Lamech's plan. As Christians, we should forgive others' transgressions more readily than the world would avenge them.

Jesus [23]If you want to understand the kingdom of heaven,
think about a king who wants to settle accounts
with his servants. [24]Just as the king began to get his

18:22 Genesis 4:23-24

accounts in order, his assistants called his attention to a slave who owed a huge sum to him—*what 100,000 laborers might earn if they worked for 100 days.* [25]The slave, *maybe an embezzler,* had no way to make restitution, so the king ordered that he, his wife, their children, and everything the family owned be sold *on the auction block*; the proceeds from the slave sale would go toward paying back the king.

[26]Upon hearing this judgment, the slave fell down, prostrated himself before the king, and begged for mercy: "Have mercy on me, and I will somehow pay you everything." [27]The king was moved by the pathos of the situation, so indeed he took pity on the servant, told him to stand up, and then forgave the debt.

[28]But the slave went and found a friend, another slave, who owed him about a hundred days' wages. "Pay me back that money," shouted the slave, throttling his friend and shaking him with threats and violence.

[29]The slave's friend fell down prostrate and begged for mercy: "Have mercy on me, and I will somehow pay you everything."

[30]But the first slave *cackled and was hard-hearted and* refused *to hear his friend's plea.* He found *a magistrate* and had his friend thrown into prison "where," he said, "you will sit until you can pay me back." [31]The other servants saw what was going on. They were upset, so they went to the king and told him everything that had happened.

[32]The king summoned the slave, *the one who had*

owed so much money, the one whose debt the king
had forgiven. The king was livid. "You slovenly
scum," he said, *seething with chilly anger*. "You
begged me to forgive your debt, and I did. 33 *What*
would be the faithful response to such latitude and
generosity? Surely—you should have shown the
same charity to a friend who was in your debt."

34 The king turned over the unmerciful slave to
his brigade of torturers, *and they had their way*
with him until he paid his whole debt. 35 And that is
what My Father in heaven will do to you, unless
you forgive each of your brothers *and each of your*
sisters from *the very cockles of* your heart.

DIVORCE AND THE GREAT COMMANDMENT

[1]After Jesus had finished His teaching about forgiveness, He left
Galilee and He went to the section of Judea on the other side of the
Jordan River. [2]Large crowds followed Him, *and when He got to
Judea,* He set about healing them.
[3]Some Pharisees—*eyeing the crowds and watching the healings—
decided that it was again time to try to trip up Jesus.* So they
approached Jesus and asked Him this tricky question *about divorce*:

Pharisees	Is it ever lawful for a man to divorce his wife?
Jesus	[4]Haven't you read that in the beginning God created humanity male and female?* *Don't you remember what the story of our creation tells us about marriage?* [5]"For this reason, a man will leave his mother and father and cleave to his wife, and the two shall become one flesh."* *If a husband and wife are indeed one flesh, how can they divorce?* [6]If a husband and wife are one flesh, *divorce would be a bloody amputation, would it not*? "What God has brought together, let no man separate."

19:4 Genesis 1:27
19:5 Genesis 2:24

The Pharisees all but grinned to themselves—they thought they had finally caught Him in a tangle, caught Him contravening the Law of the sacred Torah. If what Jesus says is true, why did Moses detail the procedures for divorce?

Pharisees [7]Why did Moses explain that if a man leaves his wife, then he must give her a certificate of divorce and send her away, free and clear of him?

Jesus [8]Moses permitted you to divorce your wives because your hearts were hard. *But divorce was an innovation, an accommodation to a fallen world.* There was no divorce at creation. [9]Listen, friends: if you leave your wife, unless there is adultery, and then marry another woman, you yourself are committing adultery. *Only if there is adultery can you divorce your wife.*

Why? Because adultery itself is the divorce. Adultery is the thing that breaks the bond of marriage. Just as an excommunication merely recognizes the fact that someone has already been removed from the people, a divorce merely legalizes what harlotry has created. But should someone leave his wife for any other reason—because he has nothing to say to her, because she continually burns his food, because she is profligate with the household resources, because he simply cannot stand the sight of her—this is outside of the message Jesus offered here. You may behave as if a marriage has been undone—indeed, you may believe that a marriage has been undone—but you are deluding yourselves. In the eyes of God, the marriage bonds still hold a man to his wife.

The disciples, who had listened and heard every word of this exchange, were shaken.

Disciples | 10 If this is how it is, then it is better to avoid marrying in the first place.

Jesus | 11 Not everyone can hear this teaching, only those to whom it has been given. 12 *Some people do not marry, of course.* Some people are eunuchs because they are born that way, others have been made eunuchs by men, and others have renounced marriage for the sake of the kingdom of heaven. Anyone who can embrace that call should do so.

13 At this, some *of Jesus' followers* brought their children before Jesus; they wanted Him to place His hands on the children and pray *for them.* Some of the disciples, *mistakenly thinking that Jesus wouldn't want to be bothered with the likes of children,* began to rebuke the crowd.

Jesus | 14 Let the little children come to Me; do not get in their way. For the kingdom of heaven belongs to children like these. 15 He laid His hands on them, *He prayed with them,* and then He left that spot *and went elsewhere.*

16 Then, a *young* man came up to Jesus.

Young Man | Teacher, what good deed can I do to assure myself eternal life?

Jesus | 17 Strange that you should ask Me what is good. There is only One who is good. If you want to participate in His *divine* life, obey the Commandments.

Young Man [18]Which Commandments *in particular*?

Jesus *Well, to begin with,* do not murder, do not commit adultery, do not steal, do not give false testimony,
[19]honor your father and mother, and love your neighbor as yourself.*

Young Man [20]I've kept those Commandments faithfully. What else do I need to do?

Jesus looked at the man and could see that he was very earnest, wanted to be taught, and wanted to know what he needed to do to participate in God's reality. Jesus knew his shoulders would sag under the weight of the next hard instruction.

Jesus [21]If you want to be perfect, go and sell all your possessions and give all your money to the poor; then you will have treasure in heaven. And then come, follow Me.

[22]The young man's *shoulders did indeed sag,* and he went away sad because he was very wealthy indeed.

Jesus [23]This is the truth: it is hard for a rich man to enter
the kingdom of heaven. [24]Yes, it is easier for a camel to go through the eye of a needle than for a rich man to enter the kingdom of God.

19:19 Exodus 20:12-17; Deuteronomy 5:16-20

25The disciples, hearing this, were stunned.

Disciples Who then can be saved?

Jesus 26People cannot save themselves. But with God, all things are possible.

Peter 27*You just told that man to leave everything and follow You.* Well, all of us have done just that. So what should we be expecting?

Jesus 28I tell you this. When *creation is consummated and*
all things are renewed, when the Son of Man sits
on His throne in glory, you who have followed Me
will also sit on thrones. There will be 12 thrones,
and you will sit and judge the twelve tribes of
Israel. 29You who have left your house and your
fields, or your brothers and sisters, or your father
and mother, or even your children, in order to follow Me, *at that time when all is renewed, you will*
receive so much more: you will receive a 100 times
what you gave up. You will inherit eternal life.
30Those who are the first will be last, and those
who are the last will be first.

CHAPTER 20

FAIR WAGES AND POSITIONS OF HONOR

Recognizing that this teaching was a tad opaque, Jesus decided to clarify the point by way of a story.

Jesus 1The kingdom of heaven is like a wealthy landowner who got up early in the morning and went out,
first thing, to hire workers to tend his vineyard.
2He agreed to pay them one denarius* for the day's
work. The workers headed to the vineyard *while
the landowner headed home to deal with some
paperwork.* 3About three hours later he went back
to the marketplace. He saw *some unemployed* men
standing around with nothing to do.

Landowner: 4*Do you need some work?* Go over to my vineyard *and join the crew there.* I'll pay you well.

So off they went, *to join the crew at the vineyard.*
5About three hours later, and then three hours after
that, *the landowner went back to the market and
saw another crew of men and hired them, too, sending them off to his vineyard and promising to pay
them well.* 6Then finally late in the afternoon, *at the
cusp of night,* the landowner walked again *through*

20:2 Equivalent to a day's wage

the marketplace, and he saw other *workers* still standing around.

Landowner: Why have you been standing here all day, doing nothing?

Workers: [7]Because no one has hired us.

Landowner: Well, you should go over to my vineyard *and put in a few moments of work.*

And off the workers went.

[8]When quitting time arrived, the landowner called to his foreman.

Landowner: Pay the workers their day's wages, beginning with the workers I hired most recently and ending with the workers who have been here all day.

[9]So the workers who had been hired just a short while before came to the foreman, and he paid them each a denarius.* [10]*Then the workers who had arrived midday came to the foreman, and he paid each of them a denarius, too.* Finally, the workers who'd been toiling since early morning came thinking they'd be paid more, but the foreman paid each of them a denarius. [11]As they received their pay, this last group of workers began to protest.

20:9 Equivalent to a day's wage

First Workers: [12]*We've been here since the crack of dawn!* And you're paying us the exact same wage that you paid the crew that just showed up. *We deserve more than they do.* We've been slogging in the heat of the sun all day—*these others haven't worked nearly as hard as we have!*

[13]The landowner *heard these protests.*

Landowner *(to the workers)*: Friends, no one has been wronged here today. *This isn't about what you deserve.* You agreed to work for a denarius, did you
not? [14]So take your money and go home. *I can give my money to whomever I please, and* it pleases me to pay
everyone the same amount of money. [15]Do you think
I don't have the right to dispose of my money as I wish? Or does my generosity somehow prick at you?

[16]*And that is your picture:* The last will be first and the first will be last.

God's glory and kingdom are His, so He is free to lavish goodness on anyone He pleases. If you feel jealous because your friend's husband seems nicer than your husband, or because your brother works no harder than you but somehow earns far more money, or because your classmate who has the intelligence of a sponge always seems to get better grades than you do, then God's generosity will indeed undo all you have come to know and expect.

[17]As Jesus was making His way to Jerusalem, He took His twelve disciples aside and *once again* told them *what was about to happen.*

Jesus | [18]We are going to Jerusalem. The Son of Man will be betrayed to the chief priests and to the teachers of the Law. He will be condemned to death, [19]and *the priests and teachers* will turn Him over to the *Romans*, who will mock Him and flog Him and crucify him. But on the third day, He will be raised from the dead, *to new resurrected life*.

[20]*As Jesus was speaking about the things that were to come,* Zebedee's wife, whose sons were among Jesus' disciples, came to Jesus with her sons and knelt down before Him to ask a favor.

Jesus | [21]What do you want?

Zebedee's Wife | When the kingdom of God is made manifest, I want one of my boys to sit at Your right hand, and one to sit at Your left hand.

Apparently, the wife of Zebedee secretly thought her sons had worked harder and sacrificed more for Jesus than the other disciples, and she secretly suspected that Jesus loved them best. She thought He would at least do the right thing and reward their hardest work and most loyal service. She also hoped that if her sons were there on the nearest, closest thrones, she could spend eternity near and close, too, clutching onto their coattails.

Jesus *(to all three)* | [22]You don't understand what you are asking. Can you drink the cup I am going to drink?

Zebedee Brothers | Of course!

Jesus | [23]Yes, you will drink from My cup, but the thrones to My right and My left are not Mine to grant. My Father has already given those seats to those for whom they were created.

[24]The other ten disciples learned what the Zebedee brothers had asked of Jesus, and they were upset.

The conversation probably went something like this:

"How sneaky!" said one disciple.

"And, really, drawing your mother into the deal . . . that's just plain low-down," said another disciple.

"Pathetic, really," said a third, who pretended to have known all along that those thrones weren't up for grabs.

[25]So Jesus called the disciples together.

Jesus | *You need some perspective here.* Do you want the Kingdom run like the Romans run their kingdom? Their rulers have great power over the people, *but God the Father doesn't play by the Romans' rules.* [26]*This is the Kingdom's logic:* whoever wants to become great must first make himself a servant; [27]whoever wants to be first must bind himself as a slave—[28]just as the Son of Man did not come to be served, but to serve and to give His life as the ransom for many.

[29]*So finally, Jesus and his disciples* left Jericho and headed for
Jerusalem; and, *of course,* a large crowd followed them. [30]Two blind
men, sitting on the roadside, heard the crowd approaching with Jesus.

Two Blind Men | Lord, have mercy on us, Son of David!

[31]The crowd rebuked them and told them to be quiet, but they shouted louder.

Two Blind Men | Lord, Son of David, have mercy on us!

Jesus *(taking the two blind men aside)* | [32]What is it that you want, *brothers*?

Two Blind Men | [33]Lord, we want to see.

[34]Jesus had compassion on them and touched their eyes. Immediately they could see, and so they followed Him.

CHAPTER 21

ENTERING INTO JERUSALEM AND THE HOUSE OF PRAYER

[1]Jesus, the disciples, and the great crowds were heading toward
Jerusalem when they came to Bethphage on the Mount of Olives.
Jesus stopped and beckoned to two of the disciples.

Jesus | [2]Go to the village over there. There you'll find a
donkey tied *to a post* and a foal beside it. Untie
them and bring them to Me. [3]If anyone *tries to stop
you,* then tell them, "The Master needs these," and
he will send *the donkey and foal* immediately.

[4]*He sent the disciples on ahead, so His entry into Jerusalem could*
fulfill what the prophet *Zechariah* had *long since* foretold:

[5]"Tell this to Zion's daughter,
'Look—your King is approaching,
Seated humbly on a donkey,
A young foal, a beast of burden.' "*

[6]So the disciples went off and followed Jesus' instructions. [7]They
brought the donkey and foal *to Jesus,* they spread their cloaks on the
animals, and Jesus sat down *on them.* [8]The great crowd followed
suit, laying their cloaks on the road. Others cut leafy branches from
the trees and scattered those *before Jesus.* [9]And the crowds went

21:5 Zechariah 9:9

before Jesus, *walked alongside Him,* and processed behind—all singing.

Crowd | Hosanna, praises to the Son of David! Blessed is He who comes in the name of the Lord! Hosanna in the highest!*

10*And that is how* Jesus entered Jerusalem: *on a lowly donkey, with crowds surrounding Him singing praises.* The people of Jerusalem, *to say the least,* noticed this strange parade. They wondered who this could be, *this humble bearded Man on a donkey who incited such songs.*

Crowd | 11This is Jesus, the prophet, from Nazareth in Galilee.

After a great parade, Jesus and His disciples walked into the temple area, and what He saw enraged Him. He saw moneychangers, buying and selling. He saw men sitting on benches, hawking doves to those who had come from the countryside to make a sacrifice. He saw that the salesmen and teachers had turned a sanctuary of worship into a place of spiritual prostitution. This was the place where Jesus came as a boy to sit with the great teachers. It was a place where His Father received the offerings of His people. It was more than Jesus could take.

12Jesus came to the temple. He drove out all those who were buying and selling. He upended the moneychangers' tables and the dove-sellers' benches.

Jesus | 13It is written, "My house will be a house of prayer

21:9 Psalm 118:26

for all people," but you have turned this house of prayer into a den of robbers.*

> Could anyone be surprised at this other side to Jesus? He has turned out to be not just a kindly teacher as we expected. Instead He is the Liberating Messiah, not to be taken lightly. In the midst of this scene filled with joy and chaos, there were extremes. Some were beginning to understand who this Man from Galilee was—the Messiah—but the rulers were having great difficulty with the disruption to their orderly world.

14Then the blind and the lame came to the temple, and Jesus
healed them. 15Rings of children circled round and sang, "Hosanna
to the Son of David." But the priests and scribes didn't understand.
When they saw the *upturned tables, the walking paralytics, and the singing children,* they were *shocked,* indignant, *and angry, and they did not understand.*

Priests and Scribes 16Do you hear what these children are saying?

Jesus Yes. Haven't you read your own psalter? "From the mouths *and souls* of infants and toddlers, *the most innocent,* You have decreed praises for Yourself."*

17At that, Jesus left *Jerusalem.* He went to Bethany, where He
spent the night.
18The next morning, Jesus went back to the city. *It was early, and,*
He was wanting breakfast, 19He stopped at a lone fig tree by the
road. The fig tree, *disappointingly,* had no figs, only leaves.

21:13 Isaiah 56:7; Jeremiah 7:11
21:16 Psalm 8:2

Jesus | May you never bear fruit again!

Immediately, the tree shriveled up. [20]The disciples were amazed.

Disciples | How did that fig tree wither so quickly?

Jesus | [21]I tell you this: if you have faith and do not doubt, then you will be able to wither a fig tree with one glance. You will be able to tell mountains to throw themselves into the ocean, and they will obey.

As Jesus said this, one or two disciples probably glanced around the shadows of the early morning, confused and afraid. Jesus had just paraded into Jerusalem and upset the vendors and leaders with His bold talk. Now He was challenging His disciples to expect the physical creation to respond to their commands and faith. But Jesus wasn't finished.

Jesus | [22]If you believe, whatever you ask for in prayer will be granted.

[23]Jesus returned to the temple and began to teach. The chief priests and elders came to Him and wanted to know who had given Him permission to disturb the temple precincts and to teach His *crazy notions in this most sacred of spots.*

Chief Priests and Elders | Who gave You the authority to do these things?

Jesus | [24]I will answer your questions if first you answer one of Mine: [25]You saw John immersing people* *for*

21:25 Literally, immersion, an act of repentance

the redemption of their sins. Did John's cleansing come from heaven, or was he simply washing people of his own whim?

The elders knew that this question was tricky—there was no simple answer. If they acknowledged that John's ritual cleansing was from heaven, Jesus would ask why they had not accepted John's authority. [26]But if they said he had dipped people simply by his own accord, they would outrage the people who believed John was a prophet.

Chief Priests and Elders [27]We don't know.

Jesus Then neither will I tell you about the authority under which I am working. [28]*But I will tell you a story, and* you can tell Me what you make of it: There was a man who had two sons. He said to his first son,

Father: Go and work in the vineyard today.

First Son: [29]No, I will not.

But later the first son changed his mind and went.
[30]Then the father went to his second son.

Father: Go and work in the vineyard today.

Second Son: Of course, Father.

But then he did not go. [31]So which of the sons did what the father wanted?

Chief Priests and Elders *(answering at once)*: The first.

Jesus: I tell you this: the tax collectors and prostitutes will enter the kingdom of God ahead of you. [32]John came to show you *the straight path,* the path to righteousness. You did not believe him, but the tax collectors and the prostitutes did. Even as you saw *the prostitutes and the tax collectors shriven and washed clean, finding their footing on the straight path to righteousness,* still you did not change your ways and believe.

[33]Here is another story: A landowner planted a vineyard, put a wall around it, fitted it with a winepress, and built a watchtower. Then he rented the vineyard and left town. [34]When harvesttime came, the landowner sent his servants to collect rent—in the form of grapes—*from his tenants.* [35]*The tenants attacked these rent-collecting servants.* They killed one, stoned another, and beat a third. [36]The *dismayed* landowner sent another band of servants *to try to collect the tax,* a larger group of servants this time, but the tenants did the same thing—*capturing, beating, killing.* [37]Finally, the landowner sent his son to the tenants, thinking, "They will at least respect my son." [38]*But the tenants knew the son was the best way to get to the landowner,* so when they saw the son approaching they said,

Tenants: This is the landowner's heir apparent! Let's kill him and take his inheritance.

Jesus

[39]And so they did—they threw him out of the vineyard and killed him. [40]What do you think the landowner will do when he comes and sees those tenants?

Chief Priests and Elders

He will eviscerate them, *to be sure*! Then he will rent the vineyard to other tenants who will pay him at harvesttime.

Jesus

[42]I wonder if any of you has ever opened your own
psalter:

> "The stone that the builders rejected
> Has become the very stone that holds up the
> entire foundation.
> This is the work of the LORD,
> And it is marvelous in our eyes."*

[43]Therefore, the kingdom of God will be taken
away from you and given to people who will tend
its *sweet* fruit *and who will give the Creator His due.*
[44]He who falls on the stone will be broken to
pieces, and he on whom the stone falls will be
crushed.*

Jesus had just confronted the spiritual leaders of the land with hard reality. They had two choices: they could believe Him and repent, or they could disbelieve Him and call His stories rabble-rousing and craziness. In their minds, the cost of believing was just too high. Everything they had—their positions and standings in the community, their worldviews, their own images of themselves—was at stake. But they couldn't openly condemn this popular Teacher of the people.

21:42 Psalm 118:22-23
21:44 Some manuscripts omit verse 44.

45 And so the chief priests and the Pharisees, *the teachers and the*
elders, knew that when Jesus told these stories He was speaking
about them. 46 *Not believing*, they looked for a way to arrest Him—*a*
stealthy way, though. They were afraid *to make too bold a move*
against Him because all the people believed He was a prophet.

MORE PARABLES AND MARRIAGE IN THE RESURRECTION

[1]Jesus went on speaking in parables.

Jesus [2]The kingdom of heaven is like a king whose son
was getting married. The king organized a great
feast, *a huge wedding banquet.* [3]*He invited everyone*
he knew. The day of the wedding arrived, and the
king sent his servants into town to track down his
guests—but *when the servants approached them*
with the king's message, they refused to come. [4]So
the king sent out another batch of servants.

King: Tell those people I've invited to come to the wedding banquet! *Tell them* I have prepared a great feast!—everything is ready!—the oxen and fattened cattle have all been butchered, *the wine is decanted, and the table is laid out just so.*

[5]*And off the servants went, and they carried the*
king's message to the errant guests—who still paid
not a whit of attention. One guest headed into his
field *to do a little surveying; one slammed the door*
in the servant's face and sat at his desk to attend to
his accounts. [6]The rest of the guests actually
turned on the servants, brutalizing them and

killing them. [7]*When he learned of this,* the king was furious. He sent his army to kill the murderers and burn their towns. [8]*But there was, of course, still a wedding to celebrate.*

King *(to his remaining servants)*: The wedding banquet is ready, but those I invited didn't rise to the occasion. [9]So go into the streets and invite anyone you see; invite everyone you meet.

[10]And the servants did just that—they went into the streets and invited everyone they met, *rich and poor*, good and bad, *high and low, sick and well.* Everyone who was invited came, and the wedding hall practically burst with guests.

[11]The king looked around the wedding party *with glee. It was a fine way to celebrate his son's marriage.* But he spotted one man who was not dressed *appropriately. In fact, he was dressed rather plainly,* in clothes not at all fitting for a fine nuptial feast.

King: [12]Kind sir, how did you get in here without a proper suit of wedding clothes?

The man was speechless *(he had been invited in off the street, after all! The king's question was confusing, even impertinent!).* [13]*Getting no response,* the king told his servants,

King: Tie him up, and throw him out into the outer darkness, where there is weeping and grinding of teeth.

Jesus | [14]For many are invited, but few are chosen.

[15]At that, the Pharisees left. They determined to trap this Jesus
with His own words—*hang Him by His own rope, you might say.*
[16]They sent a batch of students to Him, along with a group that was
loyal to Herod.

Students | Teacher, we know You are a man of integrity and You tell the truth about the way of God. We know You don't cotton to public opinion. [17]*And that is why we trust You and want You to* settle something for us: should we, *God's chosen people,* pay taxes to Caesar or not?

[18]Jesus knew these men were out to trap Him.

Jesus | You hypocrites! Why do you show up here with such a transparent trick? [19]Bring Me a coin you would use to pay tax.

Someone handed Him a denarius.* [20]*Jesus fingered the coin.*

Jesus | Of whom is this a portrait, and who owns this inscription?

Students | [21]Caesar.

Jesus | Well then, render to Caesar what is Caesar's and to God what is God's.

22:19 Equivalent to a day's wage

[22]And those *who had come hoping to trick Jesus* were confounded
and amazed. And they left Him and went away.
[23]That same day, a band of Sadducees—*a sect of Jewish aristocrats
who, among other things,* did not expect a resurrection *or anticipate
any sort of future life at all*—put their own question to Jesus.

Sadducees

[24]Teacher, *the law of* Moses teaches that if a *married*
man dies with no children, then his brother must
marry the widow and father children in his brother's name. [25]Now, we knew a family of seven brothers. The eldest brother married and died, and since
he had no children, the next brother married his
widow. [26]*And shortly thereafter, that* second brother
*died, still having fathered no children. And on and on
it happened—that poor widow kept marrying these
brothers, and they kept dying, and there were no children* from any of the seven marriages. [27]Eventually,
the wife died. [28]So now, *Teacher*, whose wife will
she be at the resurrection? *Will she have seven hus-
bands,* since they were each married to her?

Jesus

[29]You know neither God's Scriptures nor God's
power—and so your assumptions are all wrong. [30]At
the resurrection, people will neither marry nor be
given in marriage. They will be like the angels in
heaven. *They will be kith and kin, sister and brother
to everyone. They will devote themselves to praise.*
[31]A key to this resurrected life can be found *in the
words of Moses*, which you do claim to read: [32]"I am
the God of Abraham, the God of Isaac, and the God
of Jacob."* Our God is not the God of the dead. He
is the God of the living.

22:32 Exodus 3:6

[33]And again, the crowd was amazed. They were astonished at His teaching.

[34]Hearing that Jesus had silenced the Sadducees, *a group of* Pharisees met *to consider new questions that might trip up Jesus.* [35]A legal expert thought of one that would certainly stump Him.

Pharisees	[36]Teacher, of all the laws, which commandment is the greatest?
Jesus *(quoting Scripture)*	[37]"Love the LORD your God with all your heart and all your soul and all your mind."* [38]This is the first and greatest commandment. [39]And the second is nearly as important, "Love your neighbor as yourself."* [40]The rest of the Law, and all the teachings of the prophets, are but variations on these themes.

[41]Since the Pharisees were gathered together there, Jesus *took the opportunity to* pose a question of His own.

Jesus	[42]What do you think about the Christ, *the Anointed One*? Whose Son is He?
Pharisees	*But, of course,* He is the Son of David.
Jesus	[43]Then how is it that David—*whose words were surely shaped* by the Spirit—calls Him "Lord"? [44]*For in his Psalms—or perhaps you haven't opened your psalter recently*—David writes,

22:37 Deuteronomy 6:5
22:39 Leviticus 19:18

"The LORD God said to my Lord the king,
'Sit here at My right hand, *in the place of honor and power,*
And I *will gather Your enemies together, lead them in on hands and knees,* and You will rest Your feet on their backs.'"*

45How can David call his own Son Lord?

46No one had an answer to Jesus' question. And from that day forward, no one asked Him anything.

22:44 Psalm 110:1

CHAPTER 23

WOE TO THE TEACHERS OF THE LAW

1Jesus spoke to His disciples and to the crowds that had gathered
around.

Jesus

2The Pharisees and the scribes occupy the seat of
Moses. 3So you should do the things they tell you to
do—but don't do the things they do. *Mind their*
words, not their examples. For they talk about righ-
teousness and faithfulness, but they are a faithless and
unrighteous crew. 4They heap heavy burdens upon
their neighbors' backs, and they prove unwilling to
do anything to help shoulder the load. 5They are
interested, above all, in presentation: they wrap
their heads and arms in the accoutrements of
prayer, they cloak themselves with flowing, tasseled
prayer garments, 6they covet the seats of honor at
fine banquets and in the synagogue, 7and they love
it when people recognize them in the marketplace,
call them "Teacher," and beam at them.

8But you: do not let anyone call you "Rabbi." For
you are all brothers, and you have only one Teacher.
9Indeed, do not call anyone on earth "Father," for
you have only one Father, and He is in heaven.
10Neither let anyone call you "leader," for you have
one Leader—the Christ. 11If you are recognized at

all, let it be for your service. *Delight in the one who*
calls you servant. Delight in the one who does not
notice you at all. [12]For whoever exalts himself will
be humbled, and whoever humbles himself will be
exalted.

[13]Woe to you, you teachers of the Law and
Pharisees. *There is such a gulf between what you*
say and what you do. There is such a gulch between
the beauty of the sacred Scripture you claim to love
and the shape of your daily lives. You will stand
before a crowd and lock the door of the kingdom
of heaven, *right in front of everyone*; you won't
enter the Kingdom yourselves, and you prevent
others from doing so.

[[14]Woe to you, you teachers of the Law and
Pharisees. What you say is not what you do. You
steal the homes from under the widows while you
pretend to pray for them. You will suffer great con-
demnation for this.]*

[15]Woe to you Pharisees, woe to you who teach
the Law, hypocrites! You traverse hills and mountains and seas to make one convert, and then when
he does convert, you make him much more a son of
hell than you are.

[16]Woe to you who are blind but deign to lead
others. You say, "Swearing by the temple means
nothing—but he who swears by the gold in the
temple is bound by his oath." [17]Are you fools? You
must be blind! For which is greater: the gold or the
temple that makes the gold sacred? [18]You also say,
"Swearing by the altar means nothing, but he who
swears by the sacrifice on the altar is bound by his

23:14 Verse 14 is omitted from the earliest manuscripts.

oath." [19]You must be blind! Which is greater: the sacrifice or the altar that makes it sacred? [20]So anyone who swears by the altar swears by it and by the sacrifices and gifts laid upon it. [21]And anyone who swears by the temple swears by it and by the God who sanctifies it. [22]And when you swear by heaven, you are swearing by God's throne and by Him who sits upon it.

[23]So woe to you, teachers of the Law and Pharisees. You hypocrites! You tithe from *your luxuries and your spices, giving away a tenth of* your mint, your dill, and your cumin. But you have ignored the essentials of the Law: justice, mercy, faithfulness. It is practice of the latter that makes sense of the former. [24]You *hypocritical,* blind leaders. You spoon a fly from your soup and swallow a camel.

[25]Woe to you, teachers of the Law and Pharisees, you hypocrites! You remove fine layers of film and dust from the outside of a cup or bowl, but you leave the inside full of *greed and* covetousness and self-indulgence. [26]You blind Pharisee—can't you see that if you clean the inside of the cup, the outside will be clean, too?

[27]Woe to you, teachers of the Law and Pharisees, you hypocrites! You are like a grave that has been whitewashed. You look beautiful on the outside, but on the inside you are full of moldering bones and decaying rot. [28]You appear, *at first blush,* to be righteous, *selfless, and pure*, but on the inside you are *polluted,* sunk in hypocrisy and *confusion* and lawlessness.

[29]Woe to you, teachers of the Law and Pharisees, you hypocrites! You build monuments to your

dead, *you mouth pieties over the bodies of prophets,*
you decorate the graves of your righteous ancestors. [30]And you say, "If we had lived when our forefathers lived, *we would have known better*—we
would not have joined them when they rose up
against the prophets." [31]*Even when you are preening,*
you make plain that you descended from those
who murdered our prophets. [32]So, why don't you
finish what your forefathers started? [33]You are children of vipers, you *bell-dragging* snakes. You won't
escape the judgment of hell.

[34]That is why I am sending you prophets and wise
men, teachers *of breadth and depth and substance.*
You will kill some of them and crucify others. You
will flog others in your synagogues. You will pursue
them from town to town. [35]And on your heads,
stained through your hands and drenching your clothes,
my friends, will be all the righteous blood ever shed
on this earth, from the blood of innocent Abel to the
blood of Zechariah son of Berechiah whom you
murdered in the *house of the Lord,* between the
sanctuary and the altar. [36]I tell you: this generation
will bear the blood of all that has gone before.

[37]O Jerusalem, Jerusalem. You kill the prophets
whom God gives you; you stone those God sends
you. I have longed to gather your children the way
a hen gathers her chicks under her wings, but you
refuse to be gathered. [38]Surely you can see that God
has already removed His blessing from the house
of Israel. [39]I tell you this: you will not see Me again
until you say, *with the psalmist,* "Anyone who
comes in the name of the LORD will be blessed."*

23:39 Psalm 118:26

CHAPTER 24

THE END IS STILL UNFOLDING

[1]Jesus left the temple. As He was walking away, His disciples came up to Him and asked what He thought about the temple buildings.

Jesus | [2]*Look around you.* All of it will become rubble. I tell you this: not one stone will be left standing.

[3]*Later*, as Jesus was sitting on the Mount of Olives, the disciples came to Him privately.

Disciples | *You have been making these wild predictions.* Tell us, when will these things happen: *When will the temple be destroyed?* What will be the sign that You are returning? How will we know that the end of the age is upon us?

The disciples had been listening to the prophetic judgment that Jesus issued on the religious leaders. They have images of collapsing temple buildings, of prophets pursued from town to town, of floggings, and of blood-soaked garments. They can imagine themselves blood-soaked. When will this all happen, and what does it mean? In the end it comes down to the three big questions:

1. When will the temple be destroyed?
2. What will be the signs of the Messiah's return?

3. What will be the signs of the end of the age?

The questions that follow are compelling for the disciples: How will they know when all this is to come upon them? How will they know to prepare or flee?

Jesus [4]Take care that you are not deceived. [5]For many
will come in My name claiming they are the Christ,
and many poor souls will be taken in. [6]You will
hear of wars, and you will hear rumors of wars, but
you should not panic. It is inevitable, *this violent*
breaking apart of the sinful world, but remember,
the wars are not the end. *The end is still unfolding.*
[7]Nations will do battle with nations, and kingdoms
will fight neighboring kingdoms, and there will be
famines and earthquakes. [8]*But these are not the end.*
These are the birth pangs, the beginning. *The end*
is still unfolding.

[9]They will hand you over to your enemies, who
will torture you and then kill you, and you will be
hated by all nations because of Me. [10]And many
who have followed Me and claimed to love Me and
sought God's kingdom will turn away—*they will*
abandon the faith and betray and hate one another.
[11-12]The love that they had for one another will grow
cold because few will obey the law. False prophets
will appear, many will be taken in by them, and the
only thing that will grow is wickedness. *There will*
be no end to the increase of wickedness. [13]But those
who do not waver from our path and do not follow
those false prophets—those *among you* will be
saved. [14]And this good news of God's kingdom will

be preached throughout the whole world, a testimony *to all people and* all nations. Then, *beloved,*
the end, *the consummation of all things,* will come.

[15]You will remember that the prophet Daniel
predicted this—predicted the abomination that
causes desolation*—when you see the prophesied
desolation of the holy place. (Reader, take notice; it
is important that you understand this.) [16]*When you*
see this, let those in Judea flee to the mountains.
[17]If you are *relaxing* on your rooftop *one evening*
and the signs of the temple's destructions come,
don't return to your house *to rescue a book or a pet*
or a scrap of clothing. [18]If you are in the field *when*
the great destruction begins, don't return home for
a cloak. [19]Pregnant women and nursing mothers
will have the worst of it. [20]*And as for you,* pray that
your flight *to the hills* will not come on the Sabbath
or in the cold of winter. [21]For the tribulation will be
unparalleled—hardships of a magnitude that has
not been seen since creation and that will not be
seen again. [22]*Indeed the Lord God your merciful*
judge will cut this time of trial short, and this will
be done for the benefit of the elect that some
might indeed be saved—for no one could survive
the depravity for very long.

[23]*I cannot say this clearly enough: during this*
time, someone will say to you, "Look, here is the
Christ!" or "*Aren't you relieved?* Haven't you seen
the Savior *down there, around the bend, over the hill*
and dale?" Do not believe them. [24]False Christs and
false prophets will appear, and *they will know a few*

24:15 Daniel 9:27; 11:31; 12:11

tricks—they will perform great miracles, *and they will make great promises*. If it were possible, they would even deceive God's elect. 25But I am warning you ahead of time: *remember—do not fall for their lies or lines or promises. Don't let their tricks and miracles distract you.* 26If someone says, "He's out there in the desert"—do not go. And if someone says, "He's here at our house, *at our table*"—do not believe him. 27When the Son of Man comes, *He will be as visible* as lightning in the East is visible even in the West. 28And where the carcass is, there will always be vultures.

29*And as the prophets have foretold it:* after the distress *of* those days, "the sun will grow dark, the moon will be hidden, the stars will fall from the sky, and all the powers in the heavens will be dislodged and shaken *from their places*."*

30That is when the sign of the Son of Man will appear in the sky. All the nations of the earth will mourn. They will see the Son of Man coming; they will see Him powerful and glorious, *riding on chariots* of clouds in the sky. 31With a loud trumpet call, He will send out *battalions of* angels, and they will gather His *beloved faithful* elect from the four corners of creation, from one end of heaven to the other.

32Do you remember the fig tree? As soon as its twigs get tender *and greenish*, as soon as it begins to sprout leaves, you know to expect summer. 33In the same way, when you see *the wars and the suffering and the false Messiahs and the desolations*,

---

24:29 Isaiah 13:10; 34:4

you will know the Son of Man is near—right at the door. [34]I tell you this: this generation will see all these things take place before it passes away. [35]*My words are always true, and always here with you, and you can unfurl them like a banner and chant them to yourself when you think you might forget.* Heaven and earth will pass away, but My words will never pass away.

[36]*You can't predict exactly when the beginning of the end will be unleashed.* No one knows the hour or the day, not even the angels in heaven, not even the Son. Only the Father knows. [37]As it was at the time of Noah, so it will be with the coming of the Son of Man. [38]In the days before the flood, people *were busy making lives for themselves: they* were eating and drinking, marrying and giving in marriage, *making plans and having children and growing old,* until the day Noah entered the ark. [39]Those people *had no idea what was coming; they* knew nothing *about the floods* until the floods were upon them, sweeping them all away. That is how it will be with the coming of the Son of Man. [40]Two men will be plowing a field: one will be taken, and the other will be left *in the field.* [41]Two women will be *somewhere* grinding at a mill: one will be taken, and the other will be left *at the mill.*

[42]So keep watch. You don't know when your Lord will come. [43]But you should know this: If the owner of a house had known his house was about to be broken into, *he would have stayed up all night, vigilantly.* He would have kept watch, and he would have thwarted the thief. [44]So you must be

ready because you know the Son of Man will come,
but you can't know precisely when.

[45]The trustworthy servant is the one whom the
master puts in charge of *all the servants of* his
household; it is the trustworthy servant *who not
only oversees all the work, but also* ensures the servants are properly fed and cared for. [46]*And it is, of
course, crucial that a servant who is given such
responsibility performs his responsibility to his master's standards*—so when the master returns he
finds his trust has been rewarded. [47]For then the
master will put that good servant in charge of all
his possessions. [48]*But imagine that the master's
trust was misplaced,* that the supposedly responsi-
ble servant is actually a thief who says to himself,
"My master has been gone so long, *he is not possibly coming back.*" [49]Then he beats his fellow servants and dines and drinks with drunkards. [50]*Well,
when the master returns—as certainly he will—the
servant will be caught unawares.* The master will
return on a day and at an hour when he isn't
expected. [51]And he will cut his worthless servant
into pieces and throw him out *into darkness* with
the hypocrites, where there is weeping and grinding of teeth.

Matthew

Chapter 25

BRIDESMAIDS, TALENTS, AND SERVICE

Jesus 1*Or picture the kingdom of heaven this way.* The kingdom of heaven will be like ten bridesmaids who each picked up a lantern and went out to meet a certain bridegroom. 2-4Five of these women were sensible, *good with details,* and remembered to bring small flasks of oil for their lanterns. But five of them were flighty, *too caught up in the excitement of their jaunt,* and forgot to bring oil with them. 5The bridegroom did not turn up right away. Indeed, all the women, *while waiting,* found themselves falling asleep. 6And then in the middle of the night, they heard someone call, "The bridegroom is here, finally! Wake up and greet him!" 7The women got up and trimmed the wicks of their lanterns *and prepared to go greet the groom.* 8The five women who had no oil turned to their friends for help.

Ill-prepared Bridesmaids: Please give us some of your oil! Our lanterns are flickering and will go out soon.

9But the five women who'd come prepared with oil said they didn't have enough.

Prepared Bridesmaids: If we give you some of our
oil, we'll all run out too soon! You'd better go wake
up a dealer and buy your own supply.

[10]So the five *ill-prepared* women went in search of
oil to buy, and while they were gone, the groom
arrived. The five who stood ready *with their
lanterns* accompanied him to the wedding party,
and after they arrived, the door was shut.

[11]Finally, the rest of the women turned up *at the
party*. They knocked on the door.

Ill-prepared Bridesmaids: Master, open up and let
us in!

Bridegroom *(refusing)*: [12]I certainly don't know you.

And the door remained shut. [13]So stay awake; you
neither know the day nor hour *when the Son of
Man will come.* [14]*This is how it will be.* It will be like
a landowner who is going on a trip. He instructed
his slaves about caring for his property. [15]He gave
five talents to one slave, two to the next, and then
one talent to the last slave—each according to his
ability. Then the man left.

[16]Promptly the man who had been given five talents went out and bartered and sold and turned his
five talents into ten. [17]And the one who had
received two talents *went to the market and* turned
his two into four. [18]And the slave who had received
just one talent? He dug a hole in the ground and
buried his master's money there.

[19]Eventually, the master came back from his travels, *and found his slaves,* and settled up with them. [20]The slave who had been given five talents came forward and told his master how he'd turned five into ten; *then he handed the whole lot over to his master.*

Master: [21]Excellent. *You've proved yourself not only clever, but loyal.* You've executed a rather small task masterfully, so now I am going to put you in charge of something larger. *But before you go back to work,* come join my great feast and celebration.

[22]Then the slave who had been given two talents came forward and told his master how he'd turned two into four, *and he handed all four talents to his master.*

Master: [23]Excellent. *You've proved yourself not only clever, but loyal.* You've executed a rather small task masterfully, so now I am going to put you in charge of something larger. *But before you go back to work,* come join my great feast and celebration.

[24]Finally, the man who had been given one talent came forward.

Servant: Master, I know you are a hard man, *difficult in every way. You can make a healthy sum when others would fail.* You profit when other people are doing the work. You grow rich on the backs of others. [25]So I was afraid, *dug a hole,* and hid the talent in the ground. Here it is. You can have it.

26 *The master was furious.*

Master: You are a pathetic excuse for a servant! *You have disproved my trust in you and squandered my generosity. It would be better for you if you were utterly ignorant, but you don't have that excuse.* You know I am interested in making profit! 27 You could have at least put this talent in the bank—then I could have earned a little interest on it! 28 Take that one talent away, and give it to the servant who doubled my money from five to ten.

29 You see, everything was taken away from the man who had nothing, but the man who had something got even more. 30 *And as for the slave who had buried his talent in the ground?* His master ordered his slaves to tie him up and throw him outside into the utter darkness where there is miserable mourning and great fear.

31 When the Son of Man comes in all His majesty accompanied by throngs of angels, His throne will be wondrous. 32 All the nations will assemble before Him, and He will judge them, distinguishing them from one another as a shepherd isolates the sheep from the goats. 33 He will put some, the sheep, at His right hand and some, the goats, at His left. 34 Then the King will say to those on His right,

King: Come here, *you beloved*, you people whom My Father has blessed. Claim your inheritance, the Kingdom prepared for you from the beginning of creation. 35 *You shall be richly rewarded*, for when I

was hungry, you fed Me. And when I was thirsty,
you gave Me something to drink. I was alone as a
stranger, and you welcomed Me *into your homes
and into your lives.* [36]I was naked, and you gave Me
clothes to wear; I was sick, and you tended to My
needs; I was in prison, and you comforted Me.

[37]Even then, the righteous *will not have achieved
perfect understanding, and say that they don't recall
visiting Him in prison or clothing Him.*

Righteous: Master, when did we find You hungry
and give You food? When did we find You thirsty
and slake Your thirst? [38]When did we find You a
stranger and welcome You in, or find You naked
and clothe You? [39]When did we find You sick, *and
nurse You to health*? When did we visit You when
You were in prison?

King: [40]I tell you this: whenever you saw a brother
or sister hungry or cold, whatever you did to the
least of these, so you did to Me.

[41]At that, He will turn to those on His left hand.

King: Get away from Me, *you despised* people
whom My Father has cursed. *Claim your inheritance*—the pits of flaming hell where the devil and
his minions suffer. [42]For I was starving and you left
Me with no food. When I was *dry and* thirsty, you
left Me *to struggle with* nothing to drink. [43]When I
was *alone as* a stranger, you turned away from Me.

When I was *pitifully* naked, you left Me unclothed. When I was sick, *you gave Me no care.* When I was in prison, you did not comfort Me.

Unrighteous: [44]Master, when did we see You hungry and thirsty? When did we see You friendless *or homeless or excluded*? When did we see You without clothes? When did we see You sick or in jail? *When did we see* You in distress and fail to respond?

King: [45]I tell you this: *whenever you saw a brother hungry or cold, when you saw a sister weak and without friends,* when you saw the least of these and ignored their suffering, so you ignored Me.

[46]So these, *the goats,* will go off to everlasting punishment. But the beloved, *the sheep* (the righteous), will go into everlasting life.

CHAPTER 26

LAST MEAL, BETRAYAL, AND TRIAL

1And so this is what happened, *finally*. Jesus finished all His teaching, and He said to His disciples,

Jesus 2The feast of Passover begins in two days. That is
when the Son of Man is handed over to be crucified.

3*And almost as He spoke,* the chief priests were getting together
with the elders at the home of the high priest, Caiaphas. 4They
schemed *and mused* about how they could *trick Jesus,* sneak around
and capture Him, and then kill Him.

Chief Priests 5We shouldn't try to catch Him at the great public
festival. The people would riot *if they knew what
we were doing.*

6Meanwhile, Jesus was at Bethany staying at the home of Simon
the leper. 7*While He was at Simon's house,* a woman came to see Him.
She had an alabaster flask of very valuable ointment with her, and as
Jesus reclined at the table, she poured the ointment on His head.
8The disciples, seeing this scene, were furious.

Disciples This is an absolute waste! 9The woman could have
sold that ointment for lots of money, and then she

could have given it to the poor. *That money could have fed a family for months!*

[10]Jesus knew what the disciples were saying among themselves, *so He took them to task.*

Jesus | Why don't you leave this woman alone? She has done a good thing. [11]*It is good that you are concerned about the poor*, but the poor will always be with you—I will not be. [12]In pouring this ointment on My body, she has prepared Me for My burial. [13]I tell you this: the good news *of the kingdom of God* will be spread all over the world, *and wherever the good news travels,* people will tell the story of this woman and her good discipleship. And people will remember her.

[14]At that, one of the twelve, Judas Iscariot, went to the chief priests.

Judas Iscariot | [15]What will you give me to turn Him over to you?

They offered him 30 pieces of silver. [16]And from that moment, he began to watch for a chance to betray Jesus.

[17]On the first day of the Festival of Unleavened Bread, the disciples said to Jesus,

Disciples | Where would You like us to prepare the Passover meal for You?

Jesus | [18]Go into the city, find a certain man, and say to him, "The Teacher says, 'My time is near, and I am going to celebrate Passover at your house with My disciples.'"

19So the disciples *went off and* followed Jesus' instructions. *They
found the man's house, secured the owner's permission,* and got the
Passover meal ready.

20When evening came, Jesus sat down with the twelve. 21*They
praised God for redeeming His people from bondage in Egypt,* and ate
their dinner.

Jesus | I tell you this: one of you here will betray Me.

22The disciples, *of course,* were horrified.

A Disciple | Not me!

Another Disciple | *It's not me, Master, is it?*

Jesus | 23It's the one who shared this dish of food with Me.
That is the one who will betray Me. 24Just as our
sacred Scripture has taught, the Son of Man is on
His way. But there will be nothing but misery for
he who hands Him over. That man will wish he
had never been born.

25At that, Judas, who was indeed planning to betray Him, said,

Judas | It's not me, Master, is it?

Jesus | I believe you've just answered your own question.

26As they were eating, Jesus took some bread. He offered a blessing *over the bread,* and then He broke it and gave it to His disciples.

Jesus | Take this and eat; it is My body.

[27]And then He took the cup *of wine*, He made a blessing over it, and *He passed it around the table.*

Jesus | Take this and drink, all of you: [28]this is My blood of the new covenant, which is poured out for many for the forgiveness of sins. [29]But I tell you: I will not drink of the fruit of the vine again until I am with you once more, drinking in the kingdom of My Father.

[30]*The meal concluded.* Together, all the men sang a hymn *of praise and thanksgiving,* and then they took a late evening walk to the Mount of Olives.

Jesus | [31]Scripture says,

> "I shall strike the shepherd,
> And the sheep of the flock will scatter."*

Just so, each of you will stumble tonight, *stumble and fall,* on account of Me.

[32]Afterward, I will be raised up. And I will go before you to Galilee.

Peter | [33]*Lord,* maybe everyone else will *trip and* fall tonight, but I will not. *I'll be beside You. I won't falter.*

Jesus | [34]*If only that were true.* In fact, this very night, before the cock crows *in the morning,* you will deny Me three times.

26:31 Zechariah 13:7

Peter | [35]*No!* I won't deny You. Even if that means I have to die with You!

And each of the disciples echoed Peter.

Disciples | *We won't deny You, Lord. We'd rather cut off our right hands, or slice out our tongues, or even go with You to death.*

All of the disciples and Peter especially were sad and confused, and maybe a little bit prideful. They couldn't stand what they were hearing. Peter could not believe that he could ever betray his Lord. It was indeed a dark, bitter night.

[36]At that, Jesus led His disciples to the place called Gethsemane.

Jesus | I am going over there to pray. You sit here *while I'm at prayer.*

[37]Then He took Peter and the two sons of Zebedee *with Him,* and He grew sorrowful and deeply distressed.

Jesus | [38]My soul is overwhelmed with grief, to the point of death. Stay here and keep watch with Me.

[39]He walked a little farther and finally fell prostrate and prayed.

Jesus | Father, *this is the last thing I want.* If there is any way, please take this *bitter* cup from Me. Not My will, but Yours be done.

[40]When He came back to the disciples, He saw that they were
asleep. *Peter awoke a little less confident and slightly chagrined.*

Jesus *(to Peter)*: So you couldn't keep watch with Me for just one
short hour? [41]*Now maybe you're learning:* the spirit
is willing, but the body is weak. Watch and pray
and take care that you are not pulled down during
a time of testing.

[42]With that, Jesus returned *to His secluded spot* to pray again.

Jesus: Father, if there is no other way for this cup to pass
without My drinking it—*then not My will,* but
Yours be done.

[43]Again, Jesus returned to His disciples and found them asleep. Their
eyes were heavy-lidded, *and their bodies were curled like children
who've fallen asleep in their parents' laps.* [44]So Jesus left them again and
returned to prayer, praying the same sentiments with the same words.
[45]Again, He returned to His disciples.

Jesus: Well, you are still sleeping—are you getting a good
long rest? Now the time has come; the Son of Man
is just about to be given over *to the betrayers* and
the sinners. [46]Get up; we have to be going. Look,
here comes the one who's going to betray Me.

[47]There he was, Judas, one of the twelve leading a crowd of people from the chief priests and elders with swords and clubs; the
chief priests and the elders were right there, *ready to arrest* Jesus.
[48]*And Judas,* the one who intended to betray Him, had said *to the
elders and the chief priests* that he would give them a sign.

Judas | *I'll greet Him with a kiss.* And you will know that the One I kiss is the One you should arrest.

[49]So at once, he went up to Jesus.

Judas | Greetings, Teacher (he kisses Him).

Jesus | [50]My friend, do what you have come to do.

And at that, the company came and seized Him. [51]One of the men
with Jesus grabbed his sword and swung toward the high priest's
slave, slicing off his ear.

Jesus | [52]Put your sword back. People who live by the
sword die by the sword. [53]Surely you realize that if
I called on My Father, He would send 12 legions of
angels to rescue Me. [54]But if I were to do that, I
would be thwarting the scriptural story, wouldn't
I? *And we must allow the story of God's kingdom to
unfold.*

(To the crowds) [55]Why did you bring these
weapons, these clubs and bats? Did you think I
would fight you? That I would try to dodge and
escape like a common criminal? You could have
arrested Me any day, when I was teaching in the
temple, but you didn't.

[56]This scene had come together just so, so that
the prophecies in the sacred Scripture could be
fulfilled.

And at that, all the disciples ran away and abandoned Him.

[57]The crowd that had arrested Jesus took Him to Caiaphas, the

high priest. The scribes and elders had gathered *at Caiaphas's house*
and were waiting for Jesus to be delivered. [58]Peter followed Jesus
(though at some distance, *so as not to be seen*). He slipped into
Caiaphas's house and attached himself to a group of servants. And
he sat watching, waiting to see how things would unfold.

[59]The high priest and his council of advisors first produced false
evidence against Jesus—*false evidence meant to justify some charge*
and Jesus' execution. [60]But even though many men were willing to
lie, the council couldn't come up with the evidence it wanted.
Finally, two men stood up.

Two Men | [61]Look, He said, "I can destroy God's temple and rebuild it in three days." *What more evidence do you need?*

[62]Then, Caiaphas the high priest stood up and addressed Jesus.

Caiaphas | Aren't you going to respond to these charges? What exactly are these two men accusing you of?

[63]Jesus remained silent.

Caiaphas *(to Jesus)* | Under a sacred oath before the living God, tell us plainly: are You the Messiah, the Son of God?

Jesus | [64]So you *seem to be* saying. I will say this: beginning now, you will see the Son of Man sitting at the right hand of God's power and glory and coming on heavenly clouds.

[65]The high priest tore his robes *and screeched.*

Caiaphas | Blasphemy! We don't need any more witnesses—we've all just witnessed this most grievous blasphemy, *right here and now.* [66]So, gentlemen, what's your verdict?

Gentlemen | He deserves to die.

[67]Then they spat in His face and hit Him. Some of them smacked Him, slapped Him across the cheeks, [68]and jeered.

Some of the Men | Well, Messiah. Prophesy for us, if You can—who hit You? *And who is about to hit You next?*

[69]*As all this was going on in Caiaphas's chamber,* Peter was sitting in the courtyard with some servants. One of the servant girls came up to him.

Servant Girl | You were with Jesus the Galilean, *weren't you?*

[70]*And just as Jesus had predicted,* Peter denied it before everyone.

Peter | Not me! I don't know what you're talking about.

[71]He went out to stand by the gate. And as he walked past, another servant *girl recognized him.*

Another Servant Girl *(speaking to those standing around)* | That man over there—he was here with Jesus the Nazarene!

[72]Again, *just as Jesus had predicted,* Peter denied it, swearing an oath.

Peter | I don't know Him!

73 Peter then went to chat with a few of the servants. A little while
later, some other servants approached him:

Other Servants | Look, we know that you must be one of Jesus' followers. You speak like you are from the same area as His followers. You've got that tell-tale Galilean accent.

74 Cursing and swearing, *agitated veins popping up in his forehead
and his shoulders growing tense, Peter denied Him again.*

Peter | I do not know Him!

As the exclamation point left his mouth, a cock crowed. 75 And Peter
remembered. He remembered that Jesus *had looked at him with
something like pity* and said, "This very night, before the cock crows
in the morning, you will deny Me three times." And Peter went outside, *sat down on the ground,* and wept.

Matthew CHAPTER 27

PILATE SENDS JESUS TO THE CROSS

1 Eventually, the chief priests and the elders looked around and saw
that it was morning. They convened a council meeting whose sole
purpose was to hand down Jesus' death sentence. 2 They tied Jesus
up, took Him away, and handed Him over to the governor *of Judea*,
a man called Pilate.

3 Judas—the one who had betrayed Him *with a kiss for 30 pieces of*
silver—saw that Jesus had been condemned, and suddenly Judas
regretted what he had done. He took the silver back to the chief
priests and elders *and tried to return it to them*.

Judas | 4 *I can't keep this money!* I've sinned! I've betrayed an innocent Man! *His blood will be on my hands.*

> The priests and elders wanted nothing to do with Judas, and they refused to take his money.

Chief Priests and Elders | *We're through with you, friend. Feel remorseful if you like, or dance on His grave if you want*—the state of your soul is really none of our affair.

5 Judas threw down the money in the temple, went off, and
hanged himself.

6 The chief priests *looked at the silver coins* and picked them up.

Chief Priests and Elders | You know, according to the law, we can't put blood money in the temple treasury.

7 After some deliberation, they took the money and bought a plot of
land called Potter's Field—they would use it to bury foreigners, *sui-
cides, and others who were unfit for a full Jewish burial.* 8 (To this day,
the field is called Blood Field, *because it was bought with blood
money.*) 9 *And when the priests bought Potter's Field,* they *unwittingly*
fulfilled a prophecy made long ago by the prophet Jeremiah: "They
took 30 pieces of silver, the price set on the head of the Man by the
children of Israel, 10 and they gave them for the Potter's Field as the
Lord instructed."*

11 Jesus was standing before the governor, *Pilate.*

Pilate | Are you the King of the Jews?

Jesus | So you say.

12 The chief priests and the elders *stood and poured out their accusations: that Jesus was a traitor, a seditious rebel, a crazy, a would-be
Savior, and a would-be king.* Jesus stood in the stream of accusations,
but He did not respond.

Pilate | 13 Do You hear these accusations they are making against You?

14 Still Jesus said nothing, which Pilate found rather astounding—
no protests, no defense, nothing.

15 Now, the governor had a custom. During *the great Jewish festival
of* Passover, he would allow the crowd to pick one of the condemned
men, and *he, Pilate, would set the man free. Just like that. Gratuitous,*

27:10 Zechariah 11:12-13

gracious freedom. [16]At this time, they had a notorious prisoner named
Barabbas. [17]So when the crowd gathered, Pilate offered them a choice:

Pilate	Whom do you want me to free? Barabbas or Jesus, whom some call the Messiah?

> Pilate could have called our Jesus, "Jesus of Nazareth" or "Jesus the Carpenter," but said, "whom some call Messiah." It is significant that Pilate was in a position where he would pass judgment. He could determine who would live and who would die, and he was now preparing to hold court.

[18]Pilate knew the chief priests and elders hated Jesus and had delivered Him up because they envied Him.

[19]Then Pilate sat down on his judgment seat, and he received a message from his wife: "Distance yourself utterly from *the proceedings against* this righteous Man. I have had a dream about Him, a dream full of twisted sufferings—*He is innocent, I know it, and we should have nothing to do with Him.*"

[20]But the chief priests and the elders convinced the crowd to demand that Barabbas, not Jesus-*whom-some-call-the-Messiah*, be freed and that Jesus be put to death.

Pilate *(standing before the crowd)*	[21]Which of these men would you have me free?
Crowd *(shouting)*	Barabbas!
Pilate	[22]What would you have me do with this Jesus?
Crowd *(shouting)*	Crucify Him!

Pilate found himself arguing with the crowd.

Pilate | [23]Why? What crime has this Man committed?

Crowd *(responding with a shout)* | Crucify Him!

[24]*Pilate saw that he had laid his own trap. He realized that he had given the crowd a choice, the crowd had chosen, and*—unless he wanted a riot on his hands—*he now had to bow to their wishes.* So he took *a pitcher of* water, stood before the crowd, and washed his hands.

Pilate | You will see to this crucifixion, for this Man's blood *will be upon you* and not upon me. *I wash myself of it.*

Crowd | Indeed, let His blood be upon us—upon us and our children!

[26]So Pilate released Barabbas, and he had Jesus flogged and handed over to be crucified.

[27]The governor's soldiers took Jesus into a great hall, gathered a great crowd, [28]and stripped Jesus of His clothes, draping Him in a bold scarlet cloak, *the kind that soldiers sometimes wore.* [29]They gathered some thorny vines, wove them into a crown, and perched that crown upon His head. They stuck a reed in His right hand, and then they knelt before Him, *this inside-out, upside-down King. They mocked Him with catcalls.*

Soldiers | Hail, the King of the Jews!

They did not know that Jesus had already humbled Himself from His divine position long before, when He became a tiny baby in a barn.

[30]They spat on Him and whipped Him on the head with *His scepter*
of reeds, [31]and when they had their fill, they pulled off the bold scarlet cloak, dressed Him in His own simple clothes, and led Him off to
be crucified.

[32]As they were walking, they found a man called Simon of Cyrene
and forced him to carry the cross. [33]Eventually, they came to a place
called Golgotha, which means "Place of the Skull." [34]There, they
gave Him a drink—wine mixed with bitter herbs. He tasted it but
refused to drink it.

[35]And so they had Him crucified.

Let me tell you what the soldiers did as Jesus hung on the cross, what they did with those clothes that once gleamed the whitest white on a transfiguration mountaintop:

They divided the clothes off His back by drawing lots,* [36]and they
sat on the ground and watched Him *hang*. [37]They placed a sign over
His head: "This is Jesus, King of the Jews." [38]And then they crucified two thieves next to Him, one at His right hand and one at His
left hand. *These thieves were King Jesus' retinue.*

[39]Passersby shouted curses and blasphemies at Jesus. They
wagged their heads *at Him and hissed.*

Passersby	[40]You're going to destroy the temple and then rebuild it in three days? Why don't You start with saving Yourself? Come down from the cross, if You can, if You're God's Son.

27:35 Psalm 22:18

Chief Priests, Scribes, and Elders *(mocking Him)*

41-42 He saved others, but He can't save Himself. If
He's really the King of Israel, then let Him climb
down from the cross—then we'll believe Him. 43 He
claimed communion with God—well, let God save
Him, if He's God's beloved Son.

44 Even the thieves hanging to His right and left poured insults upon
Him.

45 And then, starting at noon, the entire land became dark. It was
dark for three hours. 46 In the middle of the dark afternoon, Jesus
cried out in a loud voice.

Jesus

Eli, Eli, lama sabachthani—My God, My God, why
have You forsaken Me?*

Bystanders

47 He's calling on Elijah.

48 One bystander grabbed a sponge, steeped it in vinegar, stuck it
on a reed, and gave Jesus the vinegar to drink.

Others

49 We'll see—we'll see if Elijah is going to come and
rescue Him.

50 And then Jesus cried out once more, loudly, and then He breathed
His last breath. 51 At that instant, the temple curtain was torn in half,
from top to bottom. The earth shook; rocks split in two; 52 tombs burst
open, and bodies of many sleeping holy women and men were raised
up. 53 After Jesus' resurrection, they came out of their tombs, went into
the holy city of Jerusalem, and showed themselves to people.

54 When the Centurion and soldiers who had been charged with
guarding Jesus felt the earthquake *and saw the rocks splitting and
the tombs opening,* they were, of course, terrified.

27:46 Psalm 22:1

Soldiers | He really was God's Son.

[55]A number of women, who had been devoted to Jesus and followed Him from Galilee, were present, too, watching from a distance. [56]Mary Magdalene was there, and Mary the mother of James and Joseph, and the mother of the sons of Zebedee.

[57]At evening time, a rich man from Arimathea arrived. His name was Joseph, and he had become a disciple of Jesus. [58]He went to Pilate and asked to be given Jesus' body; Pilate assented, and ordered his servants to turn Jesus' body over to Joseph. [59]So Joseph took the body, wrapped Jesus in a clean sheath of white linen, [60]and laid Jesus in his own new tomb, which he had carved from a rock. Then he rolled a great stone in front of the tomb's opening, and he went away. [61]Mary Magdalene was there, and so was the other Mary. They sat across from the tomb, *watching, remembering.*

[62]The next day, which is the day after the Preparation Day, the chief priests and the Pharisees went together to Pilate. [63]They reminded him that when Jesus was alive He had claimed that He would be raised from the dead after three days.

Chief Priests and Pharisees | [64]So please order someone to secure the tomb for at least three days. Otherwise, His disciples might sneak in and steal His body away, and then claim that He has been raised from the dead. If that happens, then we would have been better off just leaving Him alive.

Pilate | [65]You have a guard. Go and secure the grave.

[66]So they went to the tomb, sealed the stone in its mouth, and left the guard to keep watch.

CHAPTER 28

THE RESURRECTED LORD

[1]After the Sabbath, as the light of the next day, the first day of the week, crept over Palestine, Mary Magdalene and the other Mary came to the tomb *to keep vigil.* [2]Earlier, there had been an earthquake. An angel of the Lord had come down from heaven and had gone to the grave. He rolled away the stone and sat down on top of it. [3]He *veritably* glowed. He was vibrating with light. *His clothes were light, white like transfiguration,* like fresh snow. [4]The soldiers guarding the tomb were terrified. They froze like stone.

[5]The angel spoke to the women, *to Mary Magdalene and the other Mary.*

Angel of the Lord | Don't be afraid. I know you are here keeping watch for Jesus who was crucified. [6]But Jesus is not here. He was raised, just as He said He would be. Come over to the grave, and see for yourself. [7]And then, go straight to His disciples, and tell them He's been raised from the dead and has gone on to Galilee. You'll find Him there. Listen carefully to what I am telling you.

[8]The women were both terrified and thrilled, and they quickly left the tomb and went to find the disciples and give them this *outstandingly good* news. [9]But while they were on their way, they saw Jesus Himself.

Jesus *(greeting the women)* | Rejoice.

The women fell down before Him, kissing His feet and worshiping Him.

Jesus | [10]Don't be afraid. Go, and tell My brothers to go to Galilee. Tell them I will meet them there.

[11]As the women were making their way to the disciples, some of
the soldiers who had been standing guard by Jesus' tomb *recovered*
themselves, went to the city, and told the chief priests everything
that had happened—*the earthquake just after dawn, the angel, and*
the angel's commission to the Marys. [12]The chief priests gathered
together all the elders, *an emergency conference of sorts. They needed*
a plan. They decided the simplest course was bribery: they would pay
off the guards [13]and order them to say that the disciples had come in
the middle of the night and had stolen Jesus' corpse while they
slept. [14]The chief priests promised the soldiers they would run inter-
ference with the governor, so that the soldiers wouldn't be punished
for falling asleep when they were supposed to be keeping watch. [15]The
guards took the bribe and spread the story around town—and
indeed, you can still find people today who will tell you *that Jesus*
did not really rise from the dead, that it was a trick, some sort of
sleight of hand.

[16]The eleven disciples, *having spoken to the Marys,* headed to
Galilee, to the mountain where they were to meet Jesus. [17]When the
disciples saw Jesus there, many of them fell down and worshiped,
as Mary and the other Mary had done. But a few hung back. They
were not sure *(and who can blame them?). They did not know, not for*
sure, what to do or how to be.[18]Jesus came forward and addressed
His beloved disciples.

Jesus | I am here speaking with all the authority of God, *who has commanded Me to give you this commission*: [19]Go out and make disciples in all the nations. Wash them ceremonially* in the name of the *triune God*: Father, Son, and Holy Spirit. [20]Then disciple them. *Form them in the practices and postures that* I have taught you, and show them how to follow the commands I have laid down for you. And I will be with you, day after day, to the end of the ages.

28:19 Literally, immersing, in a rite of initiation and purification

Section Four // **exerpts from**

The Last Eyewitness

and

The Dust Off Their Feet

John 13

[1]Before the Passover festival began, Jesus was keenly aware
that His hour had come to depart from this world and to
return to the Father. From beginning to end, Jesus' days were
marked by His love for His people. [2]Before Jesus and His
disciples gathered for dinner, the adversary filled Judas Iscariot's heart with plans of deceit and betrayal. [3]Jesus, knowing
that He had come from God and was going away to God,
[4]stood up from dinner and removed His outer garments. He
then wrapped Himself in a towel, [5]poured water in a basin,
and began to wash the feet of the disciples, drying them with
His towel.

Simon Peter 6 *(as Jesus approaches)* Lord, are You going to wash my feet?

Jesus 7 Peter, you don't realize what I am doing, but you will understand later.

Peter 8 You will not wash my feet, now or ever!

I have to interrupt the story so you can get the whole picture. Can you imagine what it would feel like to have Jesus (the creative force behind the entire cosmos) wash your feet?

Have you ever been in a gathering where a rich and powerful person offers to fill your glass? You are thinking, "I should do this myself. How is it that someone of your stature would be willing to serve me?" But later you find yourself serving those who would view you as rich and powerful in the same ways that you were

Jesus Washing the Disciples' Feet

served. Multiply that experience by thousands, and you will have a small glimpse of this powerful expression.

My life changed that day; there was a new clarity about how I was supposed to live. I saw the world in a totally new way. The dirt, grime, sin, pain, rebellion, and torment around me were no longer an impediment to the spiritual path—it was the path.

Where I saw pain and filth, I found an opportunity to extend God's kingdom through an expression of love, humility, and service. This simple act is a metaphor for the lens that Christ gives us to see the cosmos. He sees the people, the world He created—which He loves—He sees the filth, the corruption in the world that torments us. His mission is to cleanse those whom He loves from the horrors that torment them. This is His redemptive work with feet, families, disease, famine, and our hearts.

So many of you have missed the heart of the gospel and Christ's example. When you see sin exposed in people, you shake your head and think how sad it is. Or worse you look down at these people for their rejection of God, lack of understanding, and poor morals. This is not the way of Christ. When Christ saw disease, He saw the opportunity to heal. Where He saw sin, He saw a chance to forgive and redeem. When He saw dirty feet, He saw a chance to wash them.

What do you see when you wander through the market, along the streets, on the beaches, and through the slums? Are you disgusted? Or do you seize the opportunity to expand God's reign of love in the cosmos? This is what Jesus did. The places we avoid, Jesus seeks. Now I must digress to tell a bit of the story from long before. I remember Him leading our little group of disciples into one of the most wretched places I have ever seen. It was a series of pools where the crippled and diseased would gather in hopes of being healed. The stench was unbearable, and no sane person would march into an area littered with wretched bodies

and communicable diseases. We followed Him reluctantly as He approached a crippled man on his mat and said to him, "Are you here in this place hoping to be healed?" The disabled man responded, "Kind Sir, I wait, like all of these people for the waters to stir, but I cannot walk. If I am to be healed by the waters, someone must carry me into the pool. So, the answer to Your question is yes—but I cannot be healed here unless someone will help me. Without a helping hand, someone else beats me to the water each time it is stirred." So, Jesus said, "Stand up, carry your mat and walk." At the moment Jesus uttered these words a healing energy coursed through the man and returned life to his limbs—he stood and walked for the first time in thirty-eight years (5:6-9).

It was not clear to us whether or not this man deserved this miracle. In fact, many of the disciples were disgusted by his lack of gratefulness and that he implicated Jesus to some of the Jewish authorities for healing him on the Sabbath. But God's grace is not earned; it is a beautiful gift to all of us.

When Jesus washed our feet He made an announcement to all who follow His path that life would not be about comfort, health, prosperity, and selfish pursuit.

I have gotten away from the story that was barely started. Let me back up and start almost from the beginning of the story again.

John 13

Simon Peter	6	*(as Jesus approaches)* Lord, are You going to wash my feet?
Jesus	7	Peter, you don't realize what I am doing, but you will understand later.
Peter	8	You will not wash my feet, now or ever!

Jesus If I don't wash you, you will have nothing to do with Me.

Peter 9 Then wash me but don't stop with my feet. Cleanse my hands and head as well.

Jesus 10 Listen, anyone who has bathed is clean all over except for the feet. But I tell you this, not all of you are clean.

[11]He knew the one with plans of betraying Him, which is why He said, "not all of you are clean." [12]After washing their feet and picking up His garments, He reclined at the table again.

Jesus Do you understand what I have done to you?
13 You call Me Teacher and Lord, and truly, that is
14 who I am. So, if your Lord and Teacher washes
your feet, then you should wash one another's
15 feet. I am your example; keep doing what I do.
16 I tell you the truth: an apostle is not greater than
the master. Those who are sent are not greater
17 than the One who sends them. If you know
these things, and if you put them into practice,
18 you will find happiness. I am not speaking about
all of you. I know whom I have chosen, but let
the Scripture be fulfilled that says, "The very
same man who eats My bread with Me, will
19 stab Me in the back." Assuredly, I tell you these
truths before they happen, so that when it all
20 transpires you will believe that I am. I tell you
the truth: anyone who accepts the ones I send
accepts Me. In turn, the ones who accept Me,
also accept the One who sent Me.

[21]Jesus was becoming visibly distressed.

Jesus | I tell you the truth: one of you will betray Me.

[22]The disciples began to stare at one another, wondering who
was the unfaithful disciple. [23]One disciple in particular, who
was loved by Jesus, reclined next to Him at the table. [24]Peter
motioned to the disciple at Jesus' side.

Peter | *(to the beloved disciple)* Find out who the betrayer is.

Beloved Disciple | 25 *(leaning in to Jesus)* Lord, who is it?

Jesus | 26 I will dip a piece of bread in My cup and give it to the one who will betray Me.

He dipped one piece in the cup and gave it to Judas, the son
of Simon Iscariot. [27]After this occurred, Satan entered into
Judas.

Jesus | *(to Judas)* Make haste, and do what you are going to do.

[28]No one understood Jesus' instructions to Judas. [29]Because
Judas carried the money, some thought he was being
instructed to buy the necessary items for the feast, or give
some money to the poor. [30]So Judas took his piece of bread
and departed into the night.
[31]Upon Judas' departure, Jesus spoke:

Jesus | Now the Son of Man will be glorified as God is
32 glorified in Him. If God's glory is in Him, His glory
is also in God. The moment of this astounding

	33	glory is imminent. My children, My time here is brief. You will be searching for Me, and as I told the Jews, "You cannot go where I am going."
	34	So, I give you a new command: Love each other deeply and fully. Remember the ways that I have loved you, and demonstrate your love for
	35	others in those same ways. Everyone will know you as followers of Christ if you demonstrate your love to others.
Simon Peter	36	Lord, where are You going?
Jesus		Peter, you cannot come with Me now, but later you will join Me.
Peter	37	Why can't I go now? I'll give my life for You!
Jesus	38	Will you really give your life for Me? I tell you the truth: you will deny Me three times before the rooster crows.

Ultimately, Peter was telling the truth. He was more than willing to lay down his life. But none of us understood the magnitude of the persecution and hatred that was about to be unleashed on all of us. You ask me, "Did that change the way you led and treated people in your community or outside of it? Some of us think you have an ax to grind with the Jews. What connection did this pattern of living have with Jesus' command to love? How can you reconcile your angst against the Jews and this command Christ gave you to love?"

Acts 2

A Taste of the Kingdom

1When the holy day of Pentecost came *50 days after Passover*, they were
gathered together in one place.

Picture yourself among the disciples: 2A sound roars from the sky
without warning, the roar of a violent wind, and the whole house
where you are gathered reverberates with the sound. 3Then a flame
appears, dividing into smaller flames and spreading from one person
to the next. 4All the apostles are filled with the Holy Spirit and begin
speaking in languages they've never spoken, as the Spirit empowers
them.

5*Because of the holiday,* there were devoted Jews staying as pilgrims in
Jerusalem from every nation under the sun. 6They heard the sound, and
a crowd gathered. They were amazed because each of them could hear
the group speaking in their native languages. 7They were shocked and
amazed by this.

Pilgrims | Just a minute. Aren't all of these people Galileans?
8How in the world do we all hear our native languages
being spoken? 9*Look*—there are Parthians *here*, and
Medes, Elamites, Mesopotamians, and Judeans, resi-
dents of Cappadocia, Pontus, and Asia, 10Phrygians and
Pamphylians, Egyptians and Libyans from Cyrene,
Romans including both Jews by birth and converts,
11Cretans, and Arabs. We're each, in our own languages, hearing these people talk about God's powerful deeds.

12 Their amazement became confusion as they wondered,

Pilgrims | What does this mean?

Skeptics | 13 It doesn't mean anything. They're all drunk on some fresh wine!

No matter who you were or what you may have seen, this miraculous sign of God's kingdom would have astounded you. The followers of Jesus were not known as people who drank too much wine with breakfast, but this unusual episode required some kind of explanation. Unfortunately, we can't comprehend or express what transpired on Pentecost. But this was not a novelty performance; rather, it was a taste of the kingdom of God.

14 As the twelve stood together, Peter shouted to the crowd,

Peter | Men of Judea and all who are staying here in
Jerusalem, listen. I want you to understand: 15 these
people aren't drunk as you may think. Look, it's only
nine o'clock in the morning! 16 *No, this isn't drunkenness;*
this is the fulfillment of the prophecy of Joel. 17 *Hear
what God says!*

In the last days, I will offer My Spirit to humanity as a libation.
Your children will boldly speak *the word of the Lord.*

Young warriors will see visions, and your elders will
dream dreams.
[18]Yes, in those days I shall offer My Spirit to all servants,
Both male and female, [and they will boldly speak the
word of the Lord].
[19]And in the heaven above and on the earth below,
I shall give signs *of impending judgment*: blood, fire, and
clouds of smoke.
[20]The sun will become a void of darkness, and the moon
will become blood.
Then the great and dreadful day of the Lord will arrive,
[21]And everyone who pleads using the name of the Lord
Will be liberated *into God's freedom and peace.**

[22]All of you Israelites, listen to my message: it's about
Jesus of Nazareth, a Man whom God authenticated for
you by performing in your presence powerful deeds,
wonders, and signs through Him, just as you yourselves
know. [23]This *Man, Jesus,* who came into your hands by
God's sure plan and advanced knowledge, you nailed to
a cross and killed in collaboration with lawless Gentiles.
[24]But God raised Jesus and unleashed Him from the ago-
nizing birth-pains of death, for death could not possibly
keep Jesus in its power. [25]David spoke *of Jesus'
resurrection*, saying:

The Lord is ever present with me. I will not live in
fear or abandon my calling because He guides my

2:21 Joel 2:28-32

> right hand. [26]My heart is glad; my soul rejoices; my body is safe. Who could want for more? [27]You will not abandon me to experience the suffering of a miserable afterlife. Nor leave me to rot alone. [28]Instead, You direct me on a path that leads to a beautiful life. As I walk with You the pleasures are never-ending, and I know true joy and contentment.*

[29]My fellow Israelites, I can say without question that David our ancestor died and was buried, and his tomb is with us today. [30]*David wasn't speaking of himself;* he was speaking as a prophet. *He saw with prophetic insight* that God had made a solemn promise to him: God would put one of his descendants on His throne. [31]Here's what David was seeing in advance; here's what David was talking about—the Messiah, the Liberating King, would be resurrected. *Think of David's words about* Him not being abandoned to the place of the dead nor being left to decay in the grave. [32]*He was talking about* Jesus, the One God has raised, whom all of us have seen with our own eyes and announce to you today. [33]Since Jesus has been lifted to the right hand of God—*the highest place of authority and power*—and since Jesus has received the promise of the Holy Spirit from the Father, He has now poured out what you have seen and heard here today. [34]*Remember:* David couldn't have been speaking of himself rising to the heavens when he said, "The Lord God said to my Lord, the King,

---

2:28 Psalm 16:8-11

[35]"'Sit here at My right hand, in the place of honor and power, and I will gather Your enemies together, lead them in on hands and knees, and You will rest Your feet on their backs.'"*

[36]Everyone in Israel should now realize with certainty *what God has done*: God has made Jesus both Lord and Liberating King—this same Jesus whom you crucified.

[37]When the people heard this, their hearts were pierced and they said to Peter and his fellow apostles,

Pilgrims | Our brothers, what should we do?

Peter | [38]Reconsider your lives; change your direction. Participate in the ceremonial washing* in the name of Jesus the Liberating King. Then your sins will be forgiven, and the gift of the Holy Spirit will be yours. [39]For the promise *of the Spirit* is for you, for your children, for all people—even those considered outsiders and outcasts—the Lord our God invites everyone to come to Him. Let God liberate you from this decaying culture!

Peter was pleading and offering many logical reasons to believe. [41]Whoever made a place for his message in their hearts received the ceremonial washing*; in fact, that day alone, about 3,000 people joined the disciples.

2:35 Psalm 110:1
2:38 Literally, immersion, a rite of initiation and purification
2:41 Literally, immersion, a rite of initiation and purification

[42]The community continually committed themselves to learning
what the apostles taught them, gathering for fellowship, breaking the
bread, and praying. [43]Everyone felt a sense of awe because the apostles
were doing many signs and wonders among them. [44]There was an
intense sense of togetherness among all who believed; they shared all
their material possessions in trust. [45]They sold any possessions and
goods *that did not benefit the community* and used the money to help
everyone in need. [46]They were unified as they worshiped at the temple
day after day. In homes, they broke bread and shared meals with glad
and generous hearts. [47]The new disciples praised God, and they enjoyed
the goodwill of all the people of the city. Day after day the Lord added
to their number everyone who was experiencing liberation.

Although this young and thriving church had no political influence, property, fame, or wealth, it was powerful. Its power was centered in living the gospel. The people valued one another more than any possessions. They came together as a large, passionate, healthy family where it was natural to pray and share all of life together. The kingdom of God was blossoming on earth as these lovers of God embraced the teachings of Christ. The church has since lost much of the beauty and appeal we see in Acts. It has become concerned with a desire for material possessions, cultural influence, and large congregations.